Unlocking Land Values to Finance Urban Infrastructure

Unlocking Land Values to Finance Urban Infrastructure

George E. Peterson

ISBN 978-0-8213-7709-3
eISBN: 978-0-8213-7710-9
DOI: 10.1596/978-0-8213-7709-3

Library of Congress Cataloging-in-Publication Data
Peterson, George E.
   Unlocking land values to finance urban infrastructure / George E. Peterson.
      p. cm. -- (Trends and policy options ; no. 7)
   Includes bibliographical references and index.
      ISBN 978-0-8213-7709-3 -- ISBN 978-0-8213-7710-9 (electronic)
   1. Infrastructure (Economics)--Finance. 2. Public land sales. 3. Land use, Urban. I. World Bank. II. Public-Private Infrastructure Advisory Facility. III. Title.
      HC79.C3P48 2008
      333.1'6--dc22
                                                                                    2008037307

Cover: Naylor Design, Inc.

CONTENTS

TABLES

FOREWORD

Urban growth throughout the developing world has created a challenge for financing infrastructure. Investment in infrastructure is needed to provide basic services for newly developed parts of urban areas. It is needed to meet the demand for a safer and more reliable water supply, higher standards for the removal and treatment of wastewater and solid waste, and the transportation requirements of a population whose expectations of mobility rise with household incomes. Infrastructure investment also is essential to the economic productivity of cities.

Traditionally, urban infrastructure has been financed from three sources: the operating savings of local governments, grants from higher levels of government, and borrowing. Each of these financing sources now faces constraints. Local budgets are hard pressed to finance basic operating services, including adequate maintenance of existing infrastructure. Higher levels of government must often limit grants to cities in the interest of prudent fiscal management. As decentralization policies have transferred service responsibilities downward, local governments are being asked to finance more of the urban capital budget from their own resources. Local borrowing has helped finance growth in urban infrastructure investment, but the local government revenue base is often insufficient to service a significant expansion of local government debt.

This book examines an important additional option for local infrastructure finance: capturing land value gains for public investment. Land values are highly sensitive to infrastructure investment and urban economic growth. Public works projects such as road construction, water supply, and mass transit investment produce benefits that are immediately capitalized into surrounding land values. Many cities in developing countries have underused public lands that would be more valuable if sold and converted into infrastructure assets. Tapping land values was a large part of the investment strategy of Western countries in financing urban infrastructure during the 19th century, when cities were growing most rapidly. As part of the overall financing mix, using land assets for infrastructure finance has several advantages. Most instruments of this type generate revenues upfront, making it easier to finance lumpy investment projects. Mobilizing finance from land transactions also generates price signals that increase the efficiency of urban land markets and help rationalize the urban development pattern.

Land-based financing is quickly becoming an important source of urban infrastructure finance in developing countries. Many of the cases examined in this book involve upfront revenues in the range of US$1 billion to US$3 billion, figures that are very large compared with total investment budgets and other sources of urban capital finance, such as borrowing. A great virtue of this book is that it delves into the practical workings of different instruments of land-based financing in many different country settings. From a local point of view it often is far simpler, institutionally, to sell an unused parcel of centrally located land or to charge developers an impact fee for new construction, than it is to install a complete property tax system.

If land sales, betterment fees, and developer charges can provide part of the solution to urban infrastructure finance, they also create new types of risks if implemented poorly. The very magnitude of revenue involved opens the way to potential favoritism, corruption, and abuses of government power. Governments cannot look to land-financing instruments as long-term generators of recurring revenue for their operating budgets. These are capital financing opportunities, whose revenues should be dedicated to the capital budget and used to finance a significant leap forward in infrastructure capacity.

The World Bank is committed to developing and disseminating knowledge of worldwide good practices to assist its clients in mobilizing finance through responsible use of land-financing techniques that also support efficient urban development. We need to understand more fully the workings of these instruments, whose application is accelerating at a rate we are just beginning to appreciate. There are opportunities for increasing transparency and revenues through public land auctions, for conducting land-asset inventories and strategic land asset management to free up underused assets for infrastructure finance, and for capturing for the public part of the gains in land values created by major urban infrastructure investments. As this book makes clear, land-based transactions offer rich opportunities to help close the infrastructure financing gap and to support the sustainable development of cities. The challenge for our clients is to seize these opportunities using sound principles of governance and implementation. We welcome the prospect of contributing to this important endeavor.

Katherine Sierra
Vice President, Sustainable Development
The World Bank

ACKNOWLEDGMENTS

The author would like to thank Mats Andersson, Alain Bertaud (consultant), Ellen Hamilton, Gregory Ingram (Lincoln Institute of Land Policy), Johannes Linn (Brookings Institution), Jorge Rebelo, Hiroaki Suzuki, Clemencia Torres de Mästle, and Sameh Wahba, as well as participants in seminars and review meetings in the World Bank, for valuable comments on this work and suggestions for further source material and analysis. Special appreciation is due to the peer reviewers for their encouragement and suggestions for improvement: Robert Buckley (Rockefeller Foundation), Mila Freire, and Abhas Jha. Work on the project was managed by Patricia Annez, who provided invaluable guidance on both substance and presentation. Funding was provided by the Public-Private Infrastructure Advisory Facility, whose director, Jyoti Shukla, helped to sharpen the message for the intended audience. Special thanks are due to Mercedes Aleman and Oriane Raulet for their help with Spanish and French parts of the manuscript, to Katia Nemes and Xiaofeng Li for their extraordinary assistance in all aspects of administrative support, and to Janique Racine for managing the publication process. This book was prepared under the overall direction of Abha Joshi-Ghani, sector manager, and Laszlo Lovei, director, whose support and suggestions are gratefully recognized.

ABOUT THE AUTHOR

George E. Peterson is a consultant on public finance, urban infrastructure, and urban management to the World Bank and other international organizations. He was a senior fellow in international public finance at the Urban Institute for 10 years; prior to that, he was director of the Public Finance Center of the Urban Institute. Recent publications include *Lessons for the Urban Century: Decentralized Infrastructure Finance in the World Bank* (co-author, World Bank 2008), *Financing Cities: Fiscal Responsibility and Urban Infrastructure in Brazil, China, India, Poland, and South Africa* (co-editor, World Bank and Sage Publications 2007), and *Decentralization in Asia and Latin America* (co-editor, Edward Elgar 2006). He received the Donald C. Stone award for lifetime research in intergovernmental finance and intergovernmental management from the American Society of Public Administration.

ABBREVIATIONS

ADC	Andean Development Corporation
BCDA	Bases Conversion Development Authority
BIAL	Bangalore International Airport Limited
EDU	equivalent dwelling unit
FSI	floor space index
IFC	International Finance Corporation
IMM	Istanbul Metropolitan Municipality
JLE	Jubilee Line Extension
JN-NURM	Jawaharlal Nehru National Urban Renewal Mission
MMRDA	Mumbai Metropolitan Regional Development Authority
NUCA	New Urban Communities Authority
SEZ	special economic zone
UDA	urban development authority
UDIC	urban development and investment corporation

Currencies

$A	Australian dollar
Col$	Colombian peso
DKr	Danish kroner
€	euro
F	French franc
£	British pound

£E   Egyptian pound
₱   Philippine peso
R   South African rand
Re   Indian rupee; plural = Rs; 1 crore = 10 million rupees
R$ Brazilian real
TL   Turkish lira
US$ U.S. dollar
Y   Chinese yuan

OVERVIEW

Over the next 25 years, cities in the developing world will grow by almost 2 billion people, accounting for some 90 percent of world population growth. This growth will create huge demand for infrastructure. Infrastructure investment will be required to make cities efficient locations for economic production, to provide basic services for a larger population, and to upgrade public services in line with household incomes. At the same time, population and economic growth will drive increases in urban land and property values. The ability of cities to finance the needed infrastructure will depend in large part on their ability to capture a portion of these gains and to channel them into infrastructure finance.

This book examines the various ways in which land values can be used to help pay for investment in urban infrastructure, in addition to their role as part of the property tax base. It focuses on the principles that underlie different land-based financing techniques, their efficiency in theory, and, above all, what we can learn from practical attempts to convert principles about land-based financing into practice in developing countries. Much of this practical application involves innovative use of public-private partnerships.

Land has a long history as an instrument of urban infrastructure finance. When New York City was a fledgling, it financed its first public buildings, including a ferry terminal on the East River, by selling "water lots" that included land frontage and water development rights. A few years later, when New York built its city hall, it financed construction through a further sale of water lots, this time venturing into a type of public-private partnership (or developer exaction) by agreeing to build and maintain the town dock at public expense but requiring private purchasers of water lots to fill in their sites, extending Manhattan's land area along the riverfront, and to install private wharves. When Baron Haussmann rebuilt Paris during the Second Empire, he used public powers to condemn and then acquire the land that was converted into grand avenues as well as the excess land that lay along the path of reconstruction. The excess land served as collateral for borrowing that financed new roadways, water, natural gas, and sewer lines. Land-value gains on city-acquired property were used to repay the public debt.

Land-based financing is fast becoming an important element of urban infrastructure finance in developing countries, especially in locations where cities are growing rapidly. However, the scale of land financing has attracted surprisingly little attention. Table 1 summarizes some of the land-financing cases reported in this book and compares the magnitude of financing with other sources of capital funds or total capital spending.

Is Land-Based Financing "Market Finance?"

The term "market finance" has tended to acquire a special, limited meaning when applied to investment in public infrastructure. It refers to borrowing from the private market at market rates of interest. Thus market finance of municipal infrastructure investment has come to mean financing municipal investment through borrowing—that is, borrowing from the private market on market terms. Land-based financing is another form of market finance. The sale of publicly held land to the private sector via open auction is a market transaction that raises financing on market terms. Betterment levies are designed to capture part of the increase in the market value of land attributable to infrastructure investment. Impact fees are designed to charge developers the market cost of the infrastructure expansion their development projects will necessitate. All of these instruments, when well designed, directly incorporate market principles of financing and support efficient operation of the urban land market. When poorly designed, they can distort both financial and land markets or become means of circumventing the market entirely in favor of direct planning solutions or private financial deals.

Is Land-Based Financing of Infrastructure Economically Efficient?

Underlying the use of land-based financing instruments to pay for infrastructure is *the principle that the benefits of infrastructure projects are capitalized into land values.* As long as the spatial distribution of project benefits can be internalized within a well-defined "benefit zone," it is economically efficient to finance infrastructure projects by tapping the increments in land values resulting from them. From the other side of the market,

Location and activity	Land financing amount and use of proceeds	Comparative magnitude
Cairo, Arab Rep. of Egypt: auction of desert land for new towns (May 2007, 2,100 hectares)	US$3.12 billion: to be used to reimburse costs of internal infrastructure and build connecting highway to Cairo Ring Road	117 times total urban property tax collections in country; equal to approximately 10% of total national government revenue
Cairo, Arab Rep. of Egypt: private installation of "public" infrastructure in return for free transfer of developable desert land (2005–present)	US$1.45 billion of private investment in internal and external infrastructure plus 7% of serviced land turned over to government for moderate-income housing	Will provide a range of urban infrastructure services for more than 3,300 hectares of newly developed land, without financial cost to government
Mumbai, India: auction of land in the city's new financial center (January 2006, November 2007, total 13 hectares) by Mumbai Metropolitan Regional Development Authority (MMRDA)	US$1.2 billion: to be used primarily to finance projects in metropolitan regional transportation plan	10 times MMRDA's total capital spending in fiscal 2005; 3.5 times total value of municipal bonds issued by all urban local bodies and local utilities in India in past decade
Bangalore, India: planned sale of excess land to finance access highway to new airport built under public-private partnership	US$500 million plus; on hold; land apparently will be used instead for government office buildings and government-built industrial space	Minimum land-sale proceeds were estimated to exceed considerably the costs of highway construction and acquisition of right-of-way; present status: no access road to airport

(continued)

Table 1 Magnitude of Land Financing in Select Projects of Developing Countries *(continued)*

Location and activity	Land financing amount and use of proceeds	Comparative magnitude
Istanbul, Turkey: sale of old municipal bus station and former administrative site (March and April 2007)	US$1.5 billion in auction proceeds to be dedicated to capital investment budgets	Total municipal capital spending in fiscal 2005 was US$994 million; municipal borrowing for infrastructure investment in 2005 was US$97 million
Cape Town, South Africa: sale of Victoria and Albert Waterfront property by Transnet, the parastatal transportation agency (November 2006)	US$1.0 billion, to be used to recapitalize Transnet and support its investment in core transportation infrastructure	Sale proceeds exceeded Transnet's total capital spending in fiscal 2006; equal to 17% of five-year capital investment plan prepared in 2006
Bogotá, Colombia: betterment fees, *contribución de valorización*	US$1.0 billion collected in 1997–2007; US$1.1 billion planned for 2008–15; used to finance city street and bridge improvement program	Finances 50% of street and bridge improvements; other sources of financing: US$50 million loan from the International Finance Corporation; US$300 million international, peso-linked bond issue

Source: Author.

an impact or development fee system that charges developers the market cost of the incremental infrastructure needed to support new development has been shown to be more economically efficient than a system that finances growth in infrastructure from general revenues.

Land-based financing is not a practical or desirable way to pay for the entire capital budget. However, as part of the mix of capital financing, it has significant practical advantages. Most land-financing techniques generate revenue up front, thereby reducing dependence on debt and the fiscal risks that debt financing introduces. Several land-financing techniques generate revenue *before* infrastructure investment is undertaken. Others involve borrowing during the construction period, with debt repaid from subsequent gains in land value. In developing countries where it is difficult to obtain long-term credit for urban infrastructure finance, the up-front nature of the revenue generated by land financing adds flexibility to infrastructure financing decisions.

A well-designed land-financing system also reinforces efficiency in urban land markets. Impact fees help to steer growth to where it can be accommodated most efficiently, by differentiating fee levels according to the additional infrastructure costs that must be incurred to deliver basic services to different locations. As the cases reviewed in this book make clear, land sales by public authorities to private developers typically are motivated in equal parts by the desire to generate revenue for infrastructure investment and the desire to accelerate private investment at key development nodes. They can transform an abandoned central bus station (Istanbul), reclaimed marshland (Mumbai), or highly polluting industrial plants (China) from obstacles hindering urban development to critical growth poles.

Opportunities for Public-Private Partnership

Public-private collaboration lies at the heart of land-based infrastructure finance. In fact, land-related finance may represent the biggest opportunity for private partnerships within the sphere of urban infrastructure investment. The case studies presented in this book illustrate the variety of ways in which the public and private sectors have interacted to make such financing work. The partnership approaches fall into three basic categories: (a) donation of public land to private developers in return for private investment in "public" infrastructure, (b) sale of publicly owned land to private developers, with the financial proceeds used to finance public infrastructure investment, and (c) sharing of gains in land values created by public infrastructure investment. Gains can be shared by the use of joint venture development projects involving public and private partners, by the imposition of taxes that capture part of the land-value gain accruing to private owners, or by voluntary gain-sharing agreements negotiated prior to public investment.

Implementation of Land-Financing Instruments

Many techniques have been used to tap urban land values to support infrastructure finance. This book examines their application in both developed and developing countries. Developed-country experience is pertinent, because there is a longer track record to observe and because developing countries have drawn directly on this experience in framing their own initiatives. The new cities being built in the Arab Republic of Egypt and in India are based on the new town movement in Great Britain after World War II. Betterment levies as applied in Latin America (*contribución de valorización and contribución por mejoras*) draw directly on the principles incorporated in Spanish law. Land readjustment schemes in Asia build on the experience of Japan and the Republic of Korea. Initiatives to introduce impact fees follow the planning and legal approaches used in the United States.

Betterment Levies

Betterment levies may seem to be the most direct application of land-financing principles. A robust empirical literature has corroborated the land-value gains associated with urban infrastructure projects, particularly transportation projects. A betterment levy captures part of the land-value gain attributable to infrastructure investment by imposing a one-time tax or charge on the land-value gain. Most countries in the world have experimented with betterment levies at some point, typically taxing away 30 to 60 percent of the imputed gain in land value.

Under modern conditions, betterment levies have proved to be difficult to administer. In practice, it is difficult to identify with precision, parcel by parcel, the land-value gains resulting from public works projects. The case studies recounted in this book demonstrate the large margin of error involved in estimating the impact of public works projects on the value of individual land parcels. The "tax" rates imposed by betterment levies—30 to 60 percent of the gain in parcel value attributed to public investment—are so high that both public opinion and the courts have rejected this form of infrastructure finance unless there can be greater certainty about the underlying land-value gains. For this reason, betterment levies have fallen out of favor as a significant source of revenue.

Colombia long has used the contribución de valorización, a form of betterment levy, to finance public works. However, reliance on the scheme declined drastically in the 1980s and 1990s, to the point that it became an insignificant contributor to municipal finance. The reasons for the decline were the same as found elsewhere. Gains in land value were difficult to estimate reliably. The estimation process involved high administrative costs and led to countless legal disputes. In the last several years, however, Bogotá has simplified the approach and converted the betterment levy into a general infrastructure tax associated more loosely with land-value gains. Instead of making parcel-by-parcel estimates of land-value gains due to individual investment projects, Bogotá has packaged its street and bridge improvement program into a citywide bundle of public works projects, all financed in part through a citywide valorización fee that is broadly differentiated by benefit

    Unlocking Land Values to Finance Urban Infrastructure

zone as well as other factors. The approach has allowed Bogotá to revive valorización as an effective device for financing infrastructure. The approach is being replicated throughout Colombia and is being studied for application elsewhere in Latin America, where versions of betterment laws remain on the books.

Developer Land Sales

A good deal of privatization of infrastructure investment in Western countries has taken place through the simple expedient of requiring subdivision developers to provide their own internal infrastructure and to recover their costs through land sales. As the scale of new development increases, this policy shifts an ever-larger share of total infrastructure investment to private developers. New towns or new cities represent an extreme case of internalizing both land development and infrastructure installation. New towns also introduce an additional challenge to infrastructure financing. They must be connected to the rest of the urban area by major highways, rail connectors, and trunk utility lines.

Orestad, a new town built outside of Copenhagen, is the most recent new town built in Western Europe. It is connected to central Copenhagen by a 22-kilometer automatic metro (opened in late 2003) serving 60 million passengers a year. Both the infrastructure development for the new town and the metro line are being financed primarily through land sales.

A similar approach, albeit on a much larger scale, is being implemented in Egypt, outside of Cairo. The new cities and communities outside of Cairo are expected to house more than 5.6 million residents by 2015. Massive infrastructure investments are needed for land development on this scale. Through 2005, the New Urban Communities Authority (NUCA) had provided infrastructure, at an estimated cost (in today's terms) of £E 160 per square meter, for a total cost of some US$12.5 billion. Egypt has addressed the costs of development through an evolving policy of public-private collaboration that is moving toward recognition of the market value of land. In May 2007, NUCA auctioned off substantial parcels of desert land equipped with basic infrastructure services for US$3.12 billion, more than recovering the cost of internal investment. Proceeds will be used in part to build a major highway connecting the new city to the Cairo Ring Road.

Value Capture via Project-Related Land Sale

One of the most common strategies for recovering infrastructure costs involves the sale of land whose value has been enhanced by infrastructure investment or zoning changes. If the public sector owns the land, it can internalize the benefit of public investment and capture the gains through land sales. China has financed a large part of its urban infrastructure investment in this manner. For major urban highway projects, land surrounding the highway can be transferred to a public-private development corporation. The corporation borrows against the land as collateral, finances highway construction, and then repays debt and obtains a profit by selling land after its value has been enhanced by highway access. In this way, the municipality is able to realize major infrastructure projects at no out-of-pocket cost.

In countries where most land is owned by private landowners, this technique requires that the public sector first acquire the land. If it can acquire excess land, beyond that required for infrastructure construction, it has the potential to capture land-value gains created by infrastructure investment. The rules governing this type of eminent domain have become one of the most controversial aspects of land-based financing. This book examines the case of airport construction and modernization in India, which is one of the most successful examples of public-private partnership in urban infrastructure finance. Land acquired by the state of Karnataka provided most of the economic incentive to construct the new greenfield international airport in Bangalore, which opened in April 2008. The public-private partnership, led by Siemens, built the airport at private expense. Most of the partnership's economic return will come from commercial development of land surrounding the airport. The land was given to the partnership free of charge as part of the contractual arrangement.

An attempt to sell additional land that Karnataka acquired and then use the proceeds to finance road access to the airport apparently has failed. Excess land that the state acquired originally was to be auctioned to pay for road construction. However, it now appears that government agencies are unwilling to realize the economic value of this land via sale and instead intend to use it for government offices and government-built industrial space. No progress has been made in providing highway access to the airport. The case illustrates a more general problem associated with government fragmentation. Individual agencies that have land rights often are unwilling to cede them to help finance investment outside the agency's purview.

The "taking" of private land for public infrastructure projects is controversial, especially when part of the land is not needed for the physical project. Land economists may feel that it is appropriate for the public sector to acquire land at its value, before infrastructure investment, and to use land-value gains to help finance the infrastructure project. But farmers and informal occupants have protested compensation levels. An aggressive government can act like a monopolistic developer, endowed with the power of eminent domain, intent on maximizing its revenue rather than building infrastructure. Countries all over the world are struggling to define how much of the land-value gain from public works should be captured by government, how much should belong to private landowners or de facto land occupants, and how the rules apportioning land-value gains should be decided.

Sale of Development Rights

As an alternative to the sale of land to capture incremental value generated by public infrastructure projects, public authorities can sell development rights. Development rights fall into two categories: the right to convert rural land to urban use and the right to build at greater densities than normally would be allowed by zoning rules or height restrictions. São Paulo took the approach of selling additional construction rights to help finance public investment surrounding designated growth poles within the city. An attempt to use the approach for larger-scale financing of the metro system failed because of institutional fragmentation. The metro system is financed by state government. Development rights are controlled by city government. The city has been unwilling to use its financing instrument to defray investment costs that are the responsibility of state government.

Developer Exactions and Impact Fees

Developer exactions and impact fees, unlike value capture, approach land financing from the cost side. They are one-time, up-front charges designed to recover the infrastructure costs associated with growth. Developer exactions require developers to install at their own expense the internal infrastructure needed to meet development standards or to pay for infrastructure elements provided by public authorities. Impact fees are designed to cover the *external* infrastructure costs caused by new development. Growth generates demand for systemwide expansion in infrastructure capacity for roads, water supply, wastewater removal, parks, and other facilities. Impact fees and developer exactions are designed to make growth "pay its way" by requiring developers to pay for the expansion in infrastructure capacity that growth necessitates.

Impact fees have become an important part of infrastructure finance in the United States. They are gradually being introduced in developing countries. A fully designed impact fee system requires a strong analytical base, as well as a long-term infrastructure investment plan, to differentiate accurately the impact that new development will have on infrastructure costs by location, land use, and lot and building size. A matrix of impact fees differentiated in this way can contribute significantly to the efficiency of urban development by steering growth to areas where it can be accommodated most efficiently. In the future, impact fees (or development fees) are likely to become much more significant contributors to infrastructure finance in rapidly growing urban areas of the developing world. However, the instrument will have to be simplified to capture broad differences in infrastructure costs, without the formal, detailed analysis that is becoming the standard of good practice in the United States. In Mumbai, India, it has been estimated that a 10 percent development fee, imposed on the cost of new construction, could finance as much as 40–50 percent of all regional infrastructure investment required over the next two decades.

Land Asset Management

The balance sheets of many public entities are top heavy with urban land and property assets. At the same time, the cities where the property is located suffer acute shortages of infrastructure. Under these conditions, it can make sense for public authorities to exchange land assets for infrastructure assets. They do this by selling or leasing publicly owned land and using the proceeds to finance infrastructure investment. Rather than using land-financing instruments to finance individual investment projects, public entities undertake a balance sheet adjustment, in which they modify the overall composition of publicly held assets. They increase public infrastructure assets and reduce land assets.

Land asset management of this kind can generate substantial revenues for infrastructure investment, while at the same time accelerating private development of key land parcels. This book summarizes a series of transactions, ranging from the World Trade Center in New York to the Cape Town waterfront in South Africa and from an old municipal bus station in Istanbul to a former U.S. military compound in Metro Manila. All of these sales generated revenues of US$1 billion to more than US$3 billion, dedicated primarily to infrastructure investment. The revenues are large relative both to the level of capital investment required and other potential sources of financing. As important as the revenue, however, is the policy rationale underlying the transactions. Municipal governments and infrastructure agencies are adopting more strategic methods of land asset management. A critical element in this approach is to inventory public land holdings and to compare the value of land in public use to the market value of land. Municipalities and government agencies then can divest noncore, urban landholdings in order to concentrate financial resources and managerial attention on core infrastructure.

Opportunities for National Policy and International Agencies

Land financing is just emerging as a significant part of urban infrastructure finance. The opportunities for national policy and international technical assistance to support more efficient design and implementation are numerous, such as the following:

- *Establish clear guidelines for public land auctions.* The financial amounts at stake in land auctions are large, and the difference between an efficient auction and an ad hoc auction, or no auction at all, is also large. The World Bank's assessment of urbanization in Ethiopia, for example, found that land leased at auction commanded prices 2 to 80 times higher than land sold through administrative negotiation. Egypt's land auctions have increased proceeds from land sales by a factor of more than 10:1 from previous administrative sales of similar land. International institutions have helped countries to make more efficient use of the market on the procurement side of transactions, but much more could be done to help countries make efficient use of auctions in selling land assets.

- *Prepare land asset management strategies.* Before selling land, municipalities and other public agencies should (a) carry out an inventory that identifies all publicly held land in an urban area, (b) establish the market value of all significant parcels, and (c) make strategic decisions about whether parcels should be retained in current use by government, sold to the private sector, jointly developed by public and private partners, or converted to other public use. Countries like Egypt and South Africa have established a track record for conducting this type of strategic land asset management that can be tapped as the basis for establishing policy guidelines in other countries or urban areas.

- *Establish stable and equitable rules for the exercise of eminent domain.* The most controversial, and potentially destabilizing, aspect of urban land finance involves public acquisition of private or collective land through the use of eminent domain or other compulsory powers. Abuse of public powers in land acquisition has fueled popular resistance in China, India, and other countries. Clear laws that define how eminent domain can be used, the compensation that must be paid, and the procedures by which disputes will be resolved are critical to the continuing use of this kind of land finance for infrastructure investment. By now, a good deal of experience has been accumulated in different countries on this issue, which it would be beneficial to compile and assess as preparation for national policy choices.

- *Identify workable modifications of betterment fees and impact fees as infrastructure financing instruments.* Colombia's modification of the contribución de valorización points up the importance of making practical adjustments to traditional land-financing techniques so that they are workable under modern conditions. The next challenge is likely to involve the practical application of impact fees. Cities throughout the developing world are struggling to identify the kind of development fees that can be imposed on new construction to help both to defray the costs of infrastructure investment and to reinforce desired patterns of development.

Risks and Limitations to Land Financing

Important risks and limitations are associated with land-based financing of infrastructure. Four risks in particular deserve emphasis.

Urban land markets are volatile, and recent transactions may reflect a land asset bubble. Urban land prices in developing countries cannot steadily increase at 20–30 percent a year. Prices have been volatile in the past, and they will be volatile in the future. Land prices in developing-country cities now reflect worldwide economic conditions, including the cost and availability of credit to the recycling of petro dollars. Volatility in urban land prices is part of market reality. Practical protection against this risk starts by clearly identifying proceeds from land sales as one-time capital revenues that are to be used for one-time infrastructure projects. Risk is magnified when recent trends in land prices are extrapolated to prepare future years' capital investment plans and is magnified still further if part of the receipts from land financing is allowed to trickle over to finance operating budgets.

Land sales often lack transparency and accountability. The majority of land sales are conducted off budget. There is little public accountability as to how revenues are used. The great sums of money involved invite corruption and institutional capture by the selling agency, without regard to other priorities. This risk can be mitigated by publicly releasing capital budgets and balance sheets, which report on the sources and uses of funds, including those generated by land transactions. Laws that earmark receipts from land sales for specific items in the capital budget can protect against diversion of revenues into the general operating budget.

Land sales cannot continue indefinitely. Land sales are not a permanently recurring source of capital revenue. The amount of land available for efficient disposition will vary by country and location and can be known only after an inventory and analysis have been carried out. In countries like China, where the public sector owns all urban land and can acquire new land at the urban fringe, land sales or land leasing can be a major part of infrastructure finance for 15–20 years. In other locations, municipal governments or development agencies may own only a handful of land parcels that it makes sense to sell. In these places strategies that capture part of the land-value gains due to infrastructure investment or impose development and impact fees on new construction hold more promise as continuing sources of infrastructure finance.

Land-financing techniques are instruments of capital finance. Their ultimate value depends on the quality of planning that underlies public investment. New towns or new cities may or may not be good development policy, depending on local circumstances. Municipalities can abuse land financing by acquiring land at the urban fringe without paying adequate compensation and then squander the sale proceeds on wasteful expenditures or leapfrog development. Land financing should be viewed as an important option for financing the investment needed to achieve efficient and equitable urban growth. It is not an end in itself.

Guidelines for Selecting a Land-Financing Strategy

Different land-financing techniques require different types of information and legal and analytical support to work effectively. Table 2 summarizes various instruments, organized roughly by the increasing demands they place on planning and implementation capacity and on fundamental political agreement regarding the way land-value gains from infrastructure investment should be shared.

Table 2 Land-Financing Instruments

Instrument	Description	Key requirements	Overall difficulty
Developer exactions	Developer installs on-site and neighborhood-scale infrastructure at own expense	Clear regulations; planning and implementation capacity to link developer's infrastructure to public systems	Relatively straightforward
Sale or lease of publicly held land	Public land assets are sold, with proceeds used to finance infrastructure investment	Inventory of land assets, market valuation, and strategic decisions about best use; open auctions for disposing of land that is sold	Technical competence needed for initial inventory and appraisal; can be institutionally difficult when landholding agency does not benefit directly from sale
Public-private partnership: private investment in "public" infrastructure	Developer installs "public" infrastructure in exchange for land	Same information and analysis as for land sale; can accelerate private investment in key growth poles; competitive selection procedures become critical	Simpler than many other forms of public-private partnership; danger of nontransparent or corrupt deals between public sector and developer
Betterment levies	Public sector taxes away a portion of land-value gain resulting from infrastructure projects	Difficult and costly to administer on a parcel-by-parcel basis; simplified approach adopted by Bogotá holds great promise	Most appropriate for countries with a history of betterment levies—for example, Latin American countries in Spanish tradition

(continued)

Instrument	Description	Key requirements	Overall difficulty
Impact fees	Developers pay the cost of systemwide infrastructure expansion needed to accommodate growth	Strong planning and analytical capacity needed to identify infrastructure cost implications of development at different locations; strong execution of public investment plans	Need to develop simplified approaches that capture the core concept of recovering off-site costs of growth, without overwhelming technical demands
Acquisition and sale of excess land	Public sector acquires land surrounding the infrastructure project and sells land at a profit when project is completed and land value has been enhanced	Social agreement needed on who should benefit from land-value gains resulting from public infrastructure: the original landowner, the public fiscal authority, displaced occupants, other claimants	Technically one of the most straight-forward options; the difficulty is to reach agreement on the proper exercise of eminent domain

Source: Author.

1.

INTRODUCTION TO LAND-BASED FINANCING OF URBAN INFRASTRUCTURE

Land has long served as an instrument of urban infrastructure finance. When New York City was a fledgling, it financed its first public buildings, including a ferry terminal on the East River, through the sale of "water lots" that included land frontage and water development rights. A few years later, when New York built its city hall, it financed construction through a further sale of water lots, this time venturing into a type of public-private partnership (or developer exaction), by agreeing to build and maintain the town dock at public expense but requiring private purchasers of water lots to fill in their sites, extending the land area along the riverfront, and to install private wharves (Burrows and Wallace 1999).

In London, after the Great Fire of 1666, when streets were widened during reconstruction, landowners holding property along the streets were required to pay for the public cost of expanding and paving the streets. When Baron Haussmann rebuilt Paris during the Second Empire of Napoléon III, he used land financing in a different way. The city borrowed heavily to finance the construction of grand avenues and boulevards fully equipped with water and natural gas lines and sewers. Haussmann used public powers to condemn and then acquire the land that was converted into avenues. Excess land beyond that needed for road and public works construction was acquired and used as collateral for construction loans. The value of adjacent land escalated once the boulevards were built and utility lines were installed.

Land-value gains on city-owned property were used to repay the public debt (Marchand 1993).

Variants of these same financing techniques are being used today to pay for infrastructure construction in rapidly growing cities of the developing world.

The histories of the development of New York City and Paris also reveal some of the risks associated with land-based financing of public works. New York's greatest era of city building took place after the Civil War, as the city expanded up Manhattan Island, building streets, installing water distribution and sewerage collection systems, authorizing privately built mass transit systems, and tearing down shantytowns for new development. Between 1867 and 1871, New York's municipal debt tripled, as it borrowed to finance the construction of public infrastructure. Boss Tweed, in his position as commissioner of the Department of Public Works, aggressively "privatized" the land-value benefits of this public investment. He and his associates purchased large tracts of land in the path of city expansion and then sold the land at great profit when water mains, sewers, and transportation improvements were installed. In one typical transaction, Tweed and his associates bought up the entire block bounded by Fourth Avenue, Madison Avenue, 68th Street, and 69th Street, had the city install water supply for the area, and watched the value of their land take off (Burrows and Wallace 1999, 930–31).

Haussmann's financing scheme for rebuilding Paris unraveled when the courts ruled that excess land acquired by the city for road construction, but not used for actual public works, had to be returned to the original private owners—not at its increased land value after public improvements had been completed, but at its original acquisition price. This ruling made it impossible for the city to capture the land-value gains created by public investment. The land collateral backing the city's debts disappeared, Paris went into financial crisis, and Haussmann resigned.

These issues also have echoes today. The temptation to divert into private hands the land-value gains triggered by the construction of public infrastructure is always present. Land-backed financing of infrastructure continues to be vulnerable to legal or political acts that change the rules defining how the profits from public land sales should be allocated.

Subject of the Book

This book examines the various ways that land values can be used to help pay for investments in urban infrastructure. It focuses on the principles that underlie the different financing techniques, their efficiency in theory, and, above all, what we can learn from practical attempts to convert principles about land-based financing into practice in developing countries. Much of this practical application has involved the use of public-private partnerships.

Each chapter, in addition to analysis of specific categories of financing techniques, includes a series of case studies exploring how the techniques have been applied in the field and the type of implementation issues that have arisen.

The Capital Budget

Perspective on land financing of public investment can be gained by considering the capital budget of a municipality or special development agency. Table 1.1 lays out in schematic form the organization of the capital budget.

In a "normal" capital budget—or at least the capital budget most often described in textbooks—the principal sources of funds on the revenue side of the capital budget are items 1 (operating or current account surplus), 2a (capital grants from higher-level units of government), and 3 (borrowing). These items also have received the most analytical scrutiny, as regards the efficient design of capital grants, the interaction between borrowing and future debt service that must be repaid through recurring revenues, and the types of borrowing best suited for different kinds of infrastructure investment.

Land financing involves items less often addressed in general discussions of capital budgeting: 2b (betterment levies), 2c (impact fees and developer contributions), 2d (sales of land assets), as well as a subset of 3 (borrowing backed by land collateral). All of these in their standard form are one-time receipts, typically earmarked by law for capital investment. A significant part of land financing is implemented through public-private partnerships or joint ventures, represented by item 4 in the public capital budget.

Table 1.1 Representative Capital Budget

Sources of funds (revenue)	Uses of funds (expenditure)
1. Operating budget surplus	1. Infrastructure investment: (a) water and sewer, (b) roads, and (c) other basic services
2. Capital revenues: (a) capital grants from higher level government, (b) betterment levies, (c) impact fees and developer contributions, and (d) asset sales	2. Other capital improvements
3. Borrowing	3. Investments in economic development activities
4. Capital contributions from public-private partnerships	4. Capital contributions to public-private partnerships

Source: Author.

Can Land Be a Significant Source of Infrastructure Finance?
One of the findings of the study is the sheer magnitude of revenue that is being raised from land sales and other land-financing techniques and its importance relative to other items in the capital budget. In the past few years, land-based financing of urban infrastructure has taken giant strides forward. However, most of the initiatives have advanced in ad hoc isolation, without the benefit of comparative analysis. The amount of revenue generated by land-based financing relative to other sources of financing, like market-based borrowing, has not attracted much attention.

The potential for revenue generation is illustrated by several recent land transactions discussed in the book. In 2006 and 2007, the Mumbai Metropolitan Regional Development Authority sold at auction two medium-size land parcels in Mumbai, India. Fewer than 13 hectares of land were sold for the equivalent of about US$1.2 billion. The proceeds from this land sale were targeted primarily to transportation infrastructure investment in the metropolitan region. Revenue from the land sales amounted to more than five times the annual investment budget of the Mumbai Municipal Corporation and about 3.5 times the total value of municipal bonds that have been issued in all of India over the past 12 years, despite intensive efforts by international organizations to develop the municipal bond market as a source of infrastructure finance.

In May 2007, a two-day auction of land in areas designated for new city development outside of Cairo generated US$3.12 billion in receipts, an amount equivalent to roughly 10 percent of the annual budget of the national government of the Arab Republic of Egypt and more than 100 times the annual property tax revenues of all local governments in Egypt. Over the past decade, Bogotá, Colombia, has financed 217 municipal public works projects through betterment taxation levied on land-value gains produced by the projects. In all, some US$1 billion of municipal infrastructure investment has been financed in this way. These are by no means isolated examples. In some cases land-based financing of urban infrastructure has been carried out on a much larger scale. China, for example, has financed a large part of its massive urban infrastructure investment from the sale of urban land-use rights (land leasing), either paying directly for infrastructure investment with land-sale proceeds or gradually selling off appreciated land to repay investment loans from commercial banks.

High potential for revenue generation is not by itself, of course, a conclusive argument for financing urban infrastructure investment through land-based financing. However, the case studies reviewed in this book show that land sales and other devices for capturing land-value gains often are being pursued as part of a well-designed strategy for boosting overall infrastructure investment and shaping the pattern of urban development. Many land sales are being implemented by public development agencies that have been mandated by government to divest noncore assets so that they can concentrate financial resources and management attention on investment in core infrastructure facilities. In other cases, municipal governments have looked at their balance sheets and decided that converting some publicly held land into infrastructure is the right development priority, given the economic advantages of private landownership and the shortage of infrastructure.

Is Land-Based Financing "Market Finance"?

The term "market finance" has tended to acquire a special, limited meaning when applied to investment in public infrastructure. It refers to borrowing from the private market at market rates of interest. Thus market finance of municipal infrastructure investment has come to mean financing municipal investment through borrowing—that is, borrowing from the private market, on market terms.

Land-based financing is another form of market finance. The sale of publicly held land to the private sector via open auction is a market transaction, involving market prices, that raises financing on market terms. Many of the other techniques examined in this book are also examples of market finance. Private developers recover the costs of the "public" infrastructure they build through the market sale of land parcels. Before investing in large public works initiatives, cities often negotiate with major private landholders, with the landowners agreeing to contribute substantial sums to public construction of key pieces of infrastructure (like a bridge or access highway) that will open their landholdings for profitable development.

Other land-financing techniques involve what might be called "regulated markets" and are more similar to borrowing from parastatal organizations that operate with reference to the market but not on pure market terms. This is true of techniques that capture part of the value gain created by public regulation—for example, land-value gains due to rezoning or other actions that permit higher-density development. Regulatory actions of this type are a critical part of urban land markets. The gains in market value that result from changes in development rules are real. Financing techniques that capture for the public sector part of the increment in market value due to regulatory change should be viewed as market-oriented, if not pure market, instruments.

Market-based borrowing represents market finance on the liability side of the balance sheet. It finances additions to the public capital stock by borrowing that recognizes the true cost of capital in the market. Market-based borrowing has efficiency advantages over administrative allocations of credit. Land sales that convert property assets into infrastructure at market prices involve market finance on the asset side of the balance sheet. Under current practice, market distortions in asset management are at least as substantial as market distortions in borrowing. Publicly held property seldom is priced internally to recognize the cost of capital. Public institutions tend to hold excessive quantities of property assets, especially land, because of lack of market pressure and market incentives to put the assets to remunerative use (Kaganova and McKellar 2006). When disposed of, public assets seldom are sold under competitive conditions at market prices. If the goal is to recognize the true cost of capital in infrastructure investment decisions, it is as important to introduce market principles into public asset management as it is to introduce market principles into public borrowing.

Is Land-Based Financing of Infrastructure Economically Efficient?

Underlying the use of land-based financing instruments to pay for infrastructure is *the principle that the benefits of infrastructure projects are capitalized into land values.* As long as the spatial distribution of project benefits can be internalized within a well-defined "benefit zone," it is economically efficient to finance projects by tapping the increments in land values resulting from them. When there are spillover benefits, it is still efficient to recover part of the costs by tapping land-value increments within an identifiable benefit zone.

The relationship between land-value capitalization and the costs of infrastructure supply can be interpreted as an indicator of the efficiency of infrastructure provision. When benefits, measured as capitalized land values, exceed the costs of installing infrastructure, infrastructure is being undersupplied. Public infrastructure may be constrained by lack of public financing or by the failure of public agencies to respond to demand. Table 1.2 offers an illustration from Recife, Brazil. As can be seen, the land-value gains from infrastructure investment, especially for road paving and wastewater removal, substantially exceed the costs of infrastructure supply. From the standpoint of meeting economic demand, more investment in road paving and wastewater systems is needed. Investment should continue to the point where the ratio of land-value capitalization to investment cost is 1:1, as is approximately true for water supply in Recife. It is economically efficient to tax away economic rents enjoyed by landowners as a consequence of a shortage of infrastructure in order to expand supply.

Betterment levies are instruments that seek to capture for the public sector part of the land-value gains (capitalized benefits) created by public infrastructure investment. Impact fees and developer exactions work from the opposite

Table 1.2 Land-Value Gains and Infrastructure Costs in Recife, Brazil

Service	Increase in land value (US$ per square meter) by distance to center			Ratio of gain in land value to investment cost
	5–10 kilometers	15–20 kilometers	25–30 kilometers	
Water supply	11.1	5.1	3.2	1.02
Road pavement	9.1	4.8	3.4	2.58
Wastewater removal	8.5	1.8	0.3	3.03

Source: Smolka (2007), based on Serra, Dowall, and da Motta (2003).

direction, the cost side of budgets. They recognize that private investment in new subdivision growth generates *infrastructure costs for the public sector.* The population housed in new subdivisions places demands on the regionwide network of public infrastructure, ranging from water supply and wastewater removal to road systems, schools, parks, and other categories of infrastructure. A system of land or development charges that recovers the costs of off-site infrastructure caused by new development is economically efficient both in its cost recovery and in its impact on urban spatial development. A matrix of impact fees that takes into account the actual incremental infrastructure costs associated with land development at different locations within the urbanizing region will help to steer development to those locations where it can be accommodated most efficiently.

When Is Land-Based Financing Most Appropriate?

Land-based financing of infrastructure investment has the biggest payoff where there is rapid urban growth. Under these conditions, land prices tend to rise rapidly, creating the opportunity to generate significant revenue. Rapid growth also magnifies infrastructure investment needs, requiring significant sources of development finance. In reviewing the history of developed countries like France, Japan, and the United States, it is apparent that land-based financing techniques were used most heavily during periods of rapid urban growth when there were large leaps in the scale of urban investment. The rapid urbanization now being experienced by many developing countries makes land financing attractive for them as well.

Three categories of urban infrastructure investment can be distinguished when matching financing instruments with investment needs: new developments, major capital projects, and infrastructure to support basic services.

Infrastructure Requirements of New Development
During periods of rapid urban growth, the urbanized area is expanding into the surrounding fringe, with large tracts of land being converted to urban uses by private or public developers. The magnitude of infrastructure investment required to convert raw land into urban use, and to connect new development to regionwide infrastructure networks, is easily underestimated. The scale of investment required is illustrated by some of the case studies presented in this book:

- Greater Cairo is projected to absorb an additional 5.6 million residents over the next 15 years. Given the extreme congestion of the urban core, this growth will occur at the urban fringe, in part via a national policy of new cities and new settlements development. Internal infrastructure for the new developments is expected to cost about US$32 per square meter. Egypt's New Urban Communities Authority controls 694 million square meters of land targeted for the development of new settlements. Installation of infrastructure to meet urban standards on all of this land would cost some US$21 billion. The cost estimate excludes the cost of supplying additional infrastructure in areas already designated as new cities as well as the cost of constructing major highway and rail links that will connect newly developed areas with the existing built-up region.
- The Reliance Group of India is developing a series of special economic zones (SEZs) in Navi (New) Mumbai. The estimated cost of infrastructure investment in roads, water supply and distribution, drainage and sewerage, electricity, and telecommunications networks is US$62 per square meter. The Reliance Group plans to develop a package of several SEZs, each averaging around 2,500 hectares. Total infrastructure costs per SEZ then would be more than US$1.5 billion. Again, this estimate of the infrastructure costs of land development excludes the investment required to connect the new area to the existing city, in this case via a 22.5-kilometer six-lane bridge.

Land-based financing is a natural match for financing the investment associated with new land development, whether investment is carried out by private developers or public sector agencies.

Infrastructure Financing for Major Investment Projects
Major investment projects are a second claim on land-based financing. These projects often are in the transportation sector and are a critical part of urban economic development strategy. They include major circumferential highways

or connector routes, light rail and underground rail systems, airports, seaports, and other high-profile transport initiatives. The economic benefits of these projects typically are immediately apparent and capitalized into land values. Land-based financing therefore commonly becomes one of the instruments proposed to finance the projects. The following are two examples:

- The new Crossrail commuter system was finally approved for go-ahead in London in late 2007. The project, which would cut across London and connect with Heathrow Airport and Canary Wharf, has been under intense discussion for more than two decades. Final approval was given once agreement on a financing package was reached. The financing package includes negotiated, voluntary contributions from the two largest private beneficiaries: the developers of the Canary Wharf financial district and British Airports (a private firm that operates Heathrow Airport). They are reportedly contributing between £700 million and £800 million and between £200 million and £300 million, respectively (or about US$2 billion in total), to Crossrail's financing in recognition of the impact that the rail system will have on business activity and land values.
- A committee on infrastructure, chaired by India's prime minister, has prepared a national plan for public-private airport investment. The plan has moved ahead swiftly. New greenfield international airports in Bangalore and Hyderabad were completed in spring of 2008. New airports are being constructed in other metropolitan areas, and existing airports are being expanded and modernized. Work on 11 metropolitan airports is targeted to cost about US$7.75 billion. Land financing is a critical part of the financing strategy. States are contributing land for the greenfield airports, as well as surrounding land that the private developers can use for complementary income-generating activity, thereby minimizing the public sector's cash costs. Some state agencies have acquired additional surrounding land, with the intention of financing access roads to the airports through profits from land sales.

Basic Urban Services

Investment in infrastructure for basic urban services (water supply systems, wastewater collection and treatment, drainage, street repair, and street paving) forms a third category of infrastructure investment. As table 1.2 suggests, these investments also have an impact on land values. Benefit assessment districts that tap land-value gains frequently have been used to finance this type of infrastructure and continue to be used on a small scale to finance road paving or extensions of the water system requested by neighborhoods. However, the evidence reviewed in this book suggests that the costs of administering parcel-by-parcel betterment levies can be high compared to the amount of revenue collected. This reality has contributed to a decline in their use. Municipal governments in some countries have responded by modifying the approach, so that many different investment projects are bundled together in a financing package and land-based rates are assessed across the entire city. This has rejuvenated land-based financing in parts of South America, reversing a decades-long decline in reliance on the technique for financing ordinary urban public works.

An alternative way to enlist land-based financing in support of investment in basic municipal services infrastructure has involved earmarking part of the proceeds from public land sales for the municipal capital budget or for particular items within the municipal capital budget, such as water supply and sewerage. In Ethiopia, for example, 90 percent of the proceeds of municipal land leasing, by national law, should be used to finance municipal infrastructure investment. In other settings, the fact that publicly owned land in cities is held by state or national development agencies has made it more difficult to use the profits from land sales to finance infrastructure investments that, by law, are the responsibility of municipal governments.

Land-Based Infrastructure Finance and Public-Private Partnership

Public-private collaboration lies at the heart of land-based infrastructure finance. In fact, land-related finance may represent the biggest opportunity for private partnerships within the sphere of urban infrastructure investment. Subsequent chapters illustrate the variety of ways in which the public and private sectors have interacted to make such financing work and the types of conflicts that have resulted from compulsory interaction. A summary of the basic strategies involved helps to place the case studies in context.

Public Donations of Land to Support Private Investment in Infrastructure

Public grants of land historically have been used as incentives to induce private companies to undertake infrastructure investments in the public interest. The United States built its transcontinental railroads in this way.[1] Extensive land grants were given to private railroads, in the expectation that land values would increase as regions were opened up to rail commerce, while settlement of the West would be accelerated. Several of the case studies in this book

---

[1] The federal government granted Union Pacific, Central Pacific, and Northern Pacific railroads 20 square miles of neighboring land for each mile of track laid.

make use of a similar incentive structure. Private investors in greenfield airports are given surrounding land whose value will be enhanced by international commerce flowing through the airport, or investors in urban ring roads are given the rights to land adjoining the new highways. The potential for land-value gains is part—sometimes all—of the economic reward that the public sector offers to private investors in this type of public infrastructure.

Sale of Public Land to Finance Public Infrastructure Investment

Land is the most valuable asset on the balance sheet of many municipalities and urban development agencies. The most consequential "privatization" that can take place is land sale, both in terms of revenue generation and impact on the pattern of urban development. Several of the case studies report on a new generation of "land asset management," in which government agencies sell to the private sector valuable land assets in order, first, to generate resources that they can invest in their core mandate of infrastructure provision and, second, to accelerate completion of development projects that are key to the city's economic modernization.

Sharing of Gains in Land Values Created by Public Infrastructure Investment

Many of the cases involve a sharing of land-value gains between public and private sector partners. This can be achieved by voluntary negotiation, by instruments that tax away part of the land-value gain enjoyed by private parties as a result of public investment, or by formal joint ventures, in which public agencies and private developers share the costs of, and returns to, infrastructure investment.

The Risks of Land-Based Financing

Various risks are associated with land-based financing of urban infrastructure. These risks need to be acknowledged in any program design. The following are among the principal risks.

Real estate markets are highly cyclical. The demand for land, and the price of land parcels, fluctuates violently, even in urban areas experiencing strong, long-term growth. If revenue related to land sales or developer charges is being used only to finance the infrastructure required by new development, public budgets will, to some degree, be self-correcting. Land-related revenue will decline at the same time that demand for public spending to expand infrastructure declines. If land financing is being used more broadly to finance infrastructure, however, the cyclical character of real estate markets can impose unwanted instability on the capital budget. Hong Kong, China, is an extreme example; it funds a large part of its public budget from the sale of land-leasing rights. Proceeds from land leasing fluctuated between 229 percent of expenditure on public works (and 34 percent of total government revenue) in 1997 to almost zero in 2001–03, when the government suspended all sales of land for commercial use due to lack of demand and precipitously falling land prices in the wake of the Asian financial crisis (Peterson 2007).

The large amounts of revenue generated by land sales and other techniques that capture land values invite fierce competition over the use of proceeds. Urban infrastructure investment is one claimant, but it must compete with other parties that have a stake in land values. These include farmers who want adequate compensation for land converted to urban use at the urban fringe and owners or occupants of property in "slum" areas that are displaced by publicly sponsored redevelopment. Institutions often are reluctant to relinquish proceeds from the sale of their land, with the result that revenue is not used for infrastructure investment or is used for capital investment internal to the institution, which may not be consistent with broader priorities. In the last few years, the use of public auctions for public land sales has grown rapidly, reducing somewhat the opportunity for corrupt and inefficient private transactions. However, corrupt claims on the proceeds from land sales still are common. These risks are heightened by the fact that land sales typically are conducted off budget, with little or no public accounting as to how proceeds are handled.

Faced with the potential for profit from land transactions, municipal governments and local government agencies can turn into profit-maximizing real estate developers, intent on generating the maximum revenue available. This strategy can lead to aggressive accumulation of excess land by public authorities, as has happened in China and elsewhere, promoting inefficient urban sprawl and displacement of households. The distortion of greatest consequence is the temptation to use public powers of land condemnation to overrun the claims of other parties. A government agency that has monopoly development powers can maximize profit by paying the least amount necessary to acquire land and charging the highest amount possible to sell land. This is an invitation to political abuse, unless compensation standards and other rights are protected by law.

A local government that wants to profit from land development can limit development potential through zoning or density regulations that inefficiently restrict development. Case studies in China, Japan, and the United Kingdom have reported land-price differentials of more than 100:1 for similarly situated land with and without urban development authorization (for the United Kingdom, see Barker 2004, 2006). The government then can sell development rights, exacting a high price because of the inefficient limitation of development authorization. This is primarily an urban planning issue. Sale of development rights around public transit stations or other transit nodes can be an effective way to focus development on the most efficient locations and at the same time generate funds to help pay for the infrastructure investment. Inappropriate limitations on the conversion of urban land or density of construction create artificial scarcity and the opportunity for excess public rents.

Some advocates of land-based financing have argued that essentially all urban infrastructure investment could be financed by tapping land-value gains.[2] The next chapter discusses some of the practical impediments that have made this unrealistic. The risks outlined above also make it imprudent to rely on land financing alone to pay for most of the infrastructure bill. Land-based finance is better viewed as part of the mix of urban infrastructure financing, one element in the overall capital budget.

As part of the financing mix, land-based financing has some practical advantages. Most land-financing techniques generate revenue up front, thereby reducing dependence on debt and the fiscal risks that debt financing introduces. Several land-financing techniques generate revenue *before* infra-structure investment is undertaken. Even land-financing instruments that tap land-value gains only after infrastructure construction has been completed can compress the cost recovery period. Often, it becomes possible to borrow for shorter periods and then repay the debt through land sales or other meas-ures once the infrastructure is in place. Acceleration of revenue receipts is pos-sible because land financing taps the capitalized value of expectations about *future* benefit flows. In developing countries where it is difficult to obtain long-term credits for infrastructure finance, the up-front nature of revenue generation from land financing adds significant flexibility to the overall mix of infrastructure financing.[3]

Organization of the Book

The book is divided into five chapters. Following this introduction, chapter 2 considers the principles underlying land-based financing and how these have been applied in various financing techniques used in developed countries. It highlights the kinds of public-private partnerships that have emerged and that serve as models for partnership arrangements in developing countries. Chap-ters 3 and 4 examine developing-country experience. Chapter 3 analyzes the

---

[2] Vickrey (1977), for example, has written, "The cost of public infrastructure may be defrayed at little or no expense to the general community merely by tapping the increase in land value generated by the infrastructure."

[3] Yiu (2005) emphasizes the capitalization of infrastructure "expectations" into land and hous-ing values.

application of different techniques for "benefit capture" as well as up-front obligations on developers to finance capital costs through impact fees. Value capture on the benefit side turns out to have a strong and growing role in infrastructure finance in the developing world, while developer exactions to recover infrastructure costs so far have been limited largely to internal infrastructure. The approach only recently has been expanded to cover off-site infrastructure requirements.

Chapter 4 considers the sale of publicly owned land as an infrastructure financing device. In developing countries that have private landholding regimes, public development agencies and other arms of government, including municipalities, often own a wide assortment of land and property parcels, some of them extremely valuable. One of the most pronounced trends in recent years—yet one that has passed without much notice—is a mandate for these agencies to focus on their basic mission of financing infrastructure by selling land assets. *Urban land asset management* is driven both by the magnitude of infrastructure investment that needs to be financed and by the urgency to convert key land parcels into economic development centers. Urban land asset management becomes even more critical in countries where government—usually municipal government—owns all urban land and finances a large part of the total capital budget through land leasing.

The final chapter summarizes the principal conclusions to emerge from the analysis and comparative case studies. There are lessons, in particular, for international assistance agencies and national governments wanting to help build efficient, sustainable systems of infrastructure finance that involve more private sector participation.

2.

LINKING PRINCIPLES TO LAND-FINANCE INSTRUMENTS: DEVELOPED-COUNTRY EXPERIENCE

Many techniques have been employed for tapping land values to help finance urban infrastructure investment. The rationale for these techniques often is confused and sometimes inconsistent. This chapter sorts out the relationship between benefit capitalization and cost recovery of infrastructure investments, describes a variety of land-financing techniques based on such principles, and illustrates how some of the land-based financing methods have been implemented in developed countries. Developed-country experience is pertinent, both because there often is a longer track record of implementation to observe and because developing countries have drawn directly on this experience in framing their own initiatives. The new towns being built in the Arab Republic of Egypt and India are based on the new town movement in Great Britain after World War II. Betterment taxation as applied in Latin America (*contribución de valorización* and *contribución por mejoras*) draws directly on the principles incorporated in Spanish law. Land readjustment schemes in Asia build on the experience of Japan and the Republic of Korea; initiatives to introduce impact fees follow the planning and legal approaches used in the United States.

The second part of the chapter examines another principle that underlies land-based financing of infrastructure investment: *land asset management*. Throughout the world, local governments and public agencies have turned to underused land assets as a source of revenue for infrastructure investment. They have sold land, or land-leasing rights, in order to strengthen their core mission of providing infrastructure.

Public-private partnerships are critical to the execution of both types of land financing. A wealth of experience has been accumulated regarding the elements that make for successful public-private partnerships in this arena. This experience is as valuable for the design of future programs as the implementation record of different types of land-financing instruments.

Benefit Capitalization and Value Capture

The basic rationale for using land-financing techniques to pay for urban infrastructure investment is the principle of *capitalization of benefits into land values*. Consider a simple, representative investment project: the installation of a water distribution system within a new development subdivision. The physical works are built by one agent—a public or private developer—and then turned over to an operating utility (public or private) that distributes water and charges a tariff that fully covers operating and maintenance costs.

Installation of a water supply system in the subdivision will increase land values there. The benefits that consumers assign to having access to piped water will be capitalized into land values within the access zone. The subdivision developer will be able to capture the land-value gain at the time he sells land parcels or developed lots. If there is a competitive market in land development—that is, a market where developers are free to form new subdivisions and build water distribution systems in response to demand for them—the value of the benefits of water supply that are capitalized into land values will just equal the cost of building the water system. Competition in the development market will ensure that, as long as the gains in land values from building subdivisions and water systems exceed the costs of construction, water supply coverage will be expanded to additional parcels. Community development with water access will continue to the point at which a developer just recovers his costs of infrastructure construction through higher land prices. The same principle applies to other infrastructure improvements that the developer can internalize within the subdivision (see Ingram 2007).

In this baseline case, the land developer (public or private) recovers his infrastructure costs at the time of sale of either land or developed lots. A private developer, operating in an unregulated market, will install infrastructure networks only to the extent he can fully recover his (time-adjusted) costs of investment. Informal land assemblers operating in Latin America and parts of Asia sometimes have found it more profitable to open up land parcels for sale with only the most rudimentary infrastructure, such as a few unpaved entrance roads and a handful of water sources. The benefits of further infrastructure investment, as reflected in higher land prices, are outweighed by the costs of construction, the delay in project development and land sale, and the risks of intercession by public authorities who will impose a full set of "formal sector" development standards. Public regulation that establishes minimum infrastructure standards for newly developed urban land then becomes necessary in order to protect the public from the health and congestion costs of uncontrolled development.

In the base case, one party (public or private) acts as both land developer and infrastructure investor. As long as the benefits and costs associated with infrastructure investment and land development are internalized within the development area, infrastructure costs can be financed efficiently through land sales. The model becomes more complicated, and different instruments are required for financing, when (a) the developer and infrastructure investor are not the same party, (b) benefits or costs spill over beyond the development zone, or (c) benefits are generated not by infrastructure investment but by planning or density permissions.

Financing Infrastructure through Developer Land Sales

A good deal of privatization of infrastructure investment in Western countries has taken place through the simple expedient of requiring subdivision developers to provide their own common infrastructure and to recover their costs through land sales. As the scale of new development increases, this policy shifts an ever-larger share of total infrastructure investment to private developers. New towns or new cities represent an extreme case of internalizing both land development and infrastructure installation. New towns in the developing world build directly on the experience with new towns in Great Britain (see Schafer 2006). Although the overall impact of the British new town movement is much debated, the track record in infrastructure finance is impressive. The 23 new towns that were built in Great Britain in the 1950s recovered all of their infrastructure investment costs through land and property sales, and, at the time the New Towns Development Corporation was wound up, it held excess land (serviced by infrastructure but not yet developed for housing or other use) worth more than £1 billion (Heim 1990).

New towns introduce an additional challenge for infrastructure financing. They must be connected to the rest of an urban area by major highways, rail connectors, and trunk utility lines. Orestad, a new town built outside of Copenhagen, is the most recent new town built in Western Europe. Box 2.1 recounts the history of Orestad. It involves an innovative partnership between national and local government to form a development corporation charged with land development, infrastructure construction, and land sale.

New Town Land Financing in Orestad, Denmark

Orestad is a new town outside of Copenhagen built on the precedent of British new towns. It is connected to central Copenhagen by a 22-kilometer automated metro serving 60 million passengers a year. Both the infrastructure development for the new town and construction of the metro line are being financed primarily through land sales. The metro opened in late 2003.

Orestad was planned, developed, and financed through an unusual joint venture between central and municipal government. Copenhagen originally sought central government financing for development of the new town. Instead, the government provided land amounting to 45 percent of the 310-hectare site. Copenhagen owned and contributed the other 55 percent of land. The two partners share ownership of the developer, Orestad Corporation, in proportion to their contributions of land.

Orestad's development plan called for construction of the metro line and phased development of six town centers within the overall development site. The towns were designed to be centers of education (30,000 university and technical students), corporate and commercial offices (60,000 workers), and residential housing (30,000 permanent residents). Infrastructure and metro investment has been financed by commercial rate borrowing. At the end of fiscal 2006, total debt stood at DKr 13.7 billion, or US$2.75 billion. The debt is being repaid primarily by land sales, supplemented by property taxes on new construction.

(continued)

The new town experience suggests that financing large-scale development infrastructure through land sales remains feasible, as long as the public sector owns the land scheduled for development or can acquire it cheaply. Under the Orestad model, infrastructure installation is originally financed through debt, and the debt is repaid over 20 years or more, primarily through land sales. Under different conditions, the costs of infrastructure can be recovered much more quickly. Chapter 3 shows that in Egypt, Tunisia, and other countries of North Africa and the Middle East, publicly owned land supplied with public infrastructure in new development areas can be sold to private developers at prices that far exceed the costs of infrastructure installation. This is due, on the one hand, to high demand resulting from rapid urbanization and, on the other, to bureaucratic constraints on the supply of land, which have

New Town Land Financing in Orestad, Denmark *(continued)*

In the planning stage, it was projected that land values would double on completion of the metro line. Actual market development was slower. Metro construction was delayed, and the final cost, at €1.5 billion, was double the original estimate. Land prices initially rose 10–15 percent, rather than the predicted 100 percent. However, both land prices and land sales accelerated rapidly as development proceeded and commercial occupancy began. In 2005 land approved for 224,000 square meters of gross floor space was sold; in 2006 land approved for 630,000 square meters of gross floor space was sold. Sales revenues totaled DKr 4.6 billion through the end of fiscal 2006. The Orestad Corporation now projects that all borrowing will be repaid ahead of schedule and that all infrastructure and metro construction will be financed, as planned, without government subsidy beyond the land contributions. The metro line is operated by a private company that fully recovers operating costs through fares.

Sources: Orestad Web site at the Ministry of Transportation, Denmark, http://www.trm.dk; Orestad Corporation (2005, 2006, 2007); "The Tale of Orestad and the Metro," at http://www.orestad.dk; Mikkelson (2007).

limited the amount of land in desirable locations that is supplied with infrastructure services and made available to the market.

Capturing Land-Value Gains from Private Landholders

Typically in Western countries, the landowners benefiting from public infrastructure projects are private landholders. This is true of subdivisions, when basic infrastructure is provided "free" by public authorities. It is also true of major infrastructure projects, such as the construction of expressways, metro lines, and airports. On a smaller scale, upgrading projects like road paving or the extension of water supply into unserved areas generate localized benefits that are capitalized into land prices. "Value capture" refers to techniques for capturing all or part of the increment in private land values caused by public investment. In this way, landowners who are direct beneficiaries of a project pay for part of project costs rather than taxpayers at-large.

A robust empirical literature has corroborated the land-value gains associated with urban infrastructure investment, particularly transportation projects (for a selection of this literature, see Gihring and Smith 2006; Hass-Klau

2006). For limited-access highways or rail transit systems, studies show that land-value capitalization is strongest for locations near the access points and much weaker or even negative for locations along the transportation route but distant from access points. It is typical to observe a land-price gradient, in which capitalized land-value gains fall quite steeply from the access point. For example, land-value gains associated with city metro (subway) systems have been found to be highly concentrated within a 500-meter radius of metro rail stations and largely exhausted within a 1,000-meter radius.

It is a relatively straightforward step from the observation of land-value gains due to public infrastructure investment to a recommendation that the public sector should "capture" all or part of the land-value gain caused by its investment and use the proceeds to pay for project construction. The first Habitat Conference on Human Settlements drew the following conclusion: "The rise in land values resulting from … public investment … must be subject to appropriate recapture by public bodies (United Nations 1976: rec. D.3[b]).

Many land economists have argued that almost all urban infrastructure could be paid for by value capture of this kind. The so-called Shoup Anomaly, attributed to Carl S. Shoup, asks, "Why is it so difficult to finance public infrastructure given that the increase in urban land value is much greater than the cost of the infrastructure?"

Betterment Levies

Betterment levies may seem to be the most direct form of value capture. These are charges levied directly on the increments in land value created by public investment. Most countries in the world have at one time or another experimented with variants of betterment levies. Great Britain for a period imposed a betterment levy equal to 40 percent of the land-value gain attributable to public investment. Several nations in the British Commonwealth adopted a version of this approach to land financing. Betterment levies, known as contribución de valorización or contribución por mejoras, long have been an element of infrastructure finance in Spain and were carried over to Latin America.[1]

---

[1] The Spanish system uses several instruments for capturing gains in land value. The contribución por mejoras taps gains resulting from public improvements. *Cuotas de urbanización* require land donations and infrastructure cost sharing for private developers of land receiving public planning approval for urban use. A special tax, separate from the property tax, is levied on the *increase* in land and property values; this is intended to capture part of the benefit from publicly supported urban growth. As elsewhere, revenue collection from these versions of betterment levies has been falling. See Henao González (2005).

In their basic form, betterment levies are a one-time, up-front charge on land-value gain caused by public works. In the United States, a variant in the form of special assessment districts or benefit assessment districts has been employed. These districts levy an annual charge (similar to a property tax rate) against the *increment* in land values caused by a publicly financed infrastructure project. The annual revenue flow is used to repay debt incurred to finance initial construction. During earlier periods of rapid urbanization in the United States, it was common for special assessment revenues to constitute 15 percent or more of total municipal revenues (Hagman and Misczynksi 1978).

Although the concept of betterment levies is straightforward, implementation under modern conditions has been unexpectedly difficult. A closer look at the empirical studies supporting benefit capitalization reveals some of the difficulties. Empirical analyses, even when conducted in retrospect after market price changes can be observed and in countries where data on land and property sales are regularly and consistently recorded, generally account for two-thirds or less of the observed variation in prices of land parcels. The portion of this change that can be ascribed to public infrastructure investment, though typically statistically significant, can vary between large and modest, with the exact estimate subject to a considerable range of uncertainty. Different studies of the same infrastructure project by different authors can report drastically different results. At the area level, the estimated land-value impact of an infrastructure project may differ by as much as 300 percent or even more. Variations between studies in the way aggregate land-value changes are distributed among individual parcels possessing different access and other characteristics can be still greater. If ex post empirical studies by academics are subject to such variation, it is easy to understand why administrative attempts by government to identify the land-value impacts of infrastructure projects on specific parcels of land, and to tax away 40 to 60 percent of the imputed gain from the private landowner, have been subject to challenge.

The Jubilee Line Extension (JLE) of London's underground system is a good example of the difficulty of pinpointing land-value gains. No recent infrastructure project has received more attention, in terms of potential for financing through betterment levies, than the Jubilee Line Extension. The JLE was built in the 1990s and completed shortly before Christmas 1999 at a cost of £3.5 billion (US$7 billion). Shortly after the project's completion, Don Riley published a book calling attention to the large rise in land values caused by the JLE and arguing that the project could have been financed in its entirety by betterment taxes on the land-value gains that accrued to private landowners (Riley 2002). The book commanded a good deal of notice, especially as applied to options for financing the next generation of rail projects in London.

Transport for London (the official transport agency) commissioned two large, independent studies aimed at empirically identifying the uplift in land values attributable to JLE, with the policy goal of determining whether betterment levies on land-value gains could play an important part in financing future transport initiatives. Several academic studies of JLE's land-value impacts also were launched.

The empirical results illustrate the difficulty of using betterment taxation to finance a substantial part of major infrastructure projects. One of the formally commissioned studies concluded that it was impossible to estimate land-value impacts from available data (Atisreal and Geofutures 2005). The second commissioned study warned that land-value impacts were highly uncertain and estimated that the impact on land values in Canary Wharf (the presumed primary beneficiary of the JLE) could range anywhere between £300 million and £2.7 billion (Jones Lang Lasalle 2004). A third study, carried out under the auspices of the Lincoln Institute for Land Policy, using a different methodology, estimated the land-value gain for Canary Wharf at only £40 million (Mitchell and Vickers 2003).

The uncertainty surrounding estimates of land-value gains has carried over to practical attempts to implement betterment levies. Box 2.2 summarizes efforts to introduce betterment levies in two places: Poland and Sydney, Australia.

Betterment levies have been caught in a dilemma. It has proved too ambitious in practice to try to identify with precision, parcel by parcel, the land-value gains resulting from public works projects. However, the "tax" rates imposed by betterment levies—30 to 60 percent of the gain in parcel value attributed to public investment—are so high that both public opinion and the courts have rejected this form of infrastructure finance unless there can be greater certainty about the underlying land-value gains. For this reason, betterment levies have fallen out of favor as a significant source of revenue. Practical measures to revive the use of betterment levies, discussed in chapter 3, have relaxed the strict interpretation of "value capture" and turned the betterment levy into a general infrastructure tax, more broadly tied to land-value gains.

Negotiations and Voluntary Contributions

One way of dealing with the uncertainty of price impacts, and therefore the apparent arbitrariness of the rules apportioning betterment tax burdens, is to have landowners agree on the rules for allocating costs before a project is started. This works best for small-scale projects where collective agreement is feasible. In the United States, many cities have operated systems where neighborhoods can have their streets paved whenever landowners agree to pay a

Implementation of Betterment Levies in Poland and in Sydney, Australia

Poland in 1997 passed a Land Management Act that allowed local authorities to impose "adjacency levies" on landowners, based on the market value increase of land due to installation of local public infrastructure, including roads, sewers, water supply, electricity, gas, and telecommunications. The law permitted local authorities to set betterment levy rates up to 50 percent of project costs. A majority of local governments adopted the adjacency levy at some point.

In practice, it proved extremely difficult to assess the incremental land value created by public improvements. Special appraisers were hired to estimate before-and-after land values, parcel by parcel, within improvement districts designated by the local government. However, the Supreme Administration Court set aside many of the appraisers' decisions, finding wrongful determination of land-value gains. Administrative costs were high, running as much as 30 percent of revenue collections.

A case study of Szczecin, a mid-size city of 415,000 that imposed an adjacency fee at the maximum rate of 50 percent in 2004, found that only 26 land parcels were assessed for land-value gains and that the total amount of revenue collected was equal to 0.6 percent of public infrastructure investment in the areas designated as improvement districts. The betterment statute was annulled after less than a year, primarily because the controversy over land-value determination outweighed the revenue generated.

Sydney, Australia, is one of the British Commonwealth locations that experimented with betterment levies following the example of Great Britain. Sydney's betterment levy was a variant that imposed a 30 percent tax rate on land-value gains resulting from planning authorization to convert land to urban use. Land-value gains were measured from a baseline of August 1969 to the point at which land was rezoned for urban use. All revenues generated from the betterment levy were to be used to finance infrastructure investment required for urban use, with priority given to water supply, wastewater removal, and drainage.

The New South Wales valuer-general was charged with determining the land-value gain for different parcels. Assessment was facilitated by the fact that New South Wales already had a land-value tax that required assessment of land values.

(continued)

Implementation of Betterment Levies in Poland and in Sydney, Australia
(continued)

Sydney's experiment with the betterment levy lasted a little less than five years. It generated about $A3.4 million a year on average, compared to planned annual investment in water and sewerage of $A62 million. Administrative costs averaged some 10 percent of revenue collections at the height of implementation. The betterment levy was abolished in part because landowners mounted intense political opposition and in part because the levy was generally perceived to be driving up land prices, as landowners withheld land from development in anticipation that the tax would be abolished. Revenues were viewed as modest relative to infrastructure costs and were complicated by the fact that Sydney's legislation called for revenues to go into a revolving fund that made loans (at 2 percent interest) to the public agencies responsible for investment. Sydney's version of the betterment levy further fueled controversy because it assigned all of the land-value gains between 1969 and the date of rezoning authorization to urban development planning approval, without taking into account other factors affecting land values.

Sources: Archer (1976); Gdesz (2005).

front footage rate that covers the full costs of the improvement. This approach leaves it up to landowners to determine whether their benefits exceed the costs of capital improvement. The same principle is applied in business improvement districts, where business owners agree beforehand on rules for allocating the costs of an improvement like street lighting that is in the interests of all, as long as aggregate benefits are perceived to exceed aggregate costs. The same approach is followed in countries at the other end of the income scale. Kebeles—neighborhood communities—and business districts in Ethiopia, for example, use almost exactly the same methods of reaching community agreement on the desirability of street paving or street lighting. They agree on a formula for allocating costs, which typically incorporates land size or land value as an indicator of benefit received, and then collectively pay for the community's share of the public work. In Tigray Province of Ethiopia the kebele share of street paving costs typically is set at 50 percent (see Peterson 2005).

The principle of negotiated agreement can be extended to larger works. One of the conclusions to flow from the analyses of the Jubilee Line Extension in London is that it is impractical to finance major rail investments through betterment taxation. The next large project, Crossrail, which establishes an east-west rail link across the British capital connecting outlying towns, Canary Wharf, the City of London, and Heathrow Airport, was finally approved for go-ahead in November 2007 after many years of debate over financing. The financing solution involves a capital contribution from national government, a capital contribution from the City of London, a supplement on the property tax from business property owners, and "voluntary," negotiated contributions from the two major landholders and project beneficiaries. The developers of Canary Wharf and the British Airport Authority (a private company that operates Heathrow Airport) reportedly have agreed to contribute a combined £1 billion (US$2 billion) to capital financing of the project. Although the payments are relatively modest compared to total project cost, they were necessary to finalize the cost-sharing agreement. Similarly, the real estate developer, DLF, has agreed with the Delhi (India) metro authority to finance on its own a 4-kilometer extension of the metro line to serve its Mall of India project, at an estimated cost of US$100 million.

Public Land Acquisition and Resale

Another method of avoiding arbitrary imputation of land-value gains is for the public sector to own the land around an infrastructure project and then sell it on completion of the project. If the land is sold at competitive, arm's-length terms, the sale will capture for the public sector the full value of the land, including the increment created by the construction of infrastructure. In one version of this model, the public sector acquires from the private sector the land to be used for an infrastructure project as well as surrounding land that will benefit from the increase in value caused by the public works. The difference in land values between the acquisition price and the sale price represents the value created by the infrastructure project and is captured by public authorities when the land parcels are sold on project completion.

Sale of publicly acquired land "solves" the problem of land valuation at the project completion stage. However, it introduces three other problems. First, how should land be valued at the point at which public authorities acquire it? Legal rules typically give public authorities the right to condemn land and acquire it from private parties in order to execute infrastructure projects. However, the price that should be paid is subject to varying legal rules. In most advanced countries with private freehold ownership, public authorities now must pay "market value" for land that is acquired from private parties through condemnation. Legal rules specify the procedures for determining market value. Conceptually, the primary issue is how much, if any, of the incremental value anticipated from future public infrastructure development should be capitalized into the acquisition price that public authorities pay. In other words, does the land-value gain belong to private landowners, the government, or both? This issue has been hotly contested in developed nations. As chapter 3 makes clear, an even greater range of law and practice governs the pricing of public land acquisition in developing countries.

A second issue concerns the amount of land that public authorities can acquire through condemnation. At one end of the spectrum, public authorities may be allowed to acquire only the land specifically required for construction of public works. At the other end of the spectrum, public authorities may have the latitude to acquire, at favorable prices, large amounts of surrounding land whose value will appreciate due to infrastructure construction. Most Western nations now tightly restrict the "excess" land that public authorities can acquire through condemnation. However, the law was more flexible during the periods of rapid urbanization in the nineteenth century.

Finally, how should the profits from the sale of public land be allocated? Should some of the profits realized go back to the original landowners, if they were forced to sell their holdings at current-use value or administrative prices? Should the profits from public land transactions be dedicated to financing the infrastructure projects that generated them, or should they be available for broader public use? Various allocation rules have been devised for splitting the land-value increments resulting from the installation of infrastructure. In Japan and Korea, these rules resulted in formal land readjustment schemes, in which public authorities acquired undeveloped land at current-use value, installed infrastructure systems, and then returned well-defined proportions of the finished land to the original developers, in effect splitting the land-value gains between the public and private sectors (for a recent review of international experience with land readjustment, see Hong and Needham 2007). These arrangements have fallen out of favor, as landowners today are unwilling to entrust land to government for the long periods required for urban development, and government is reluctant to pay the high prices now necessary to acquire land ready for urbanization. Land readjustment has left its mark on developing-country practice, however, especially in Asia.

Box 2.3 summarizes the classic case of public land acquisition and infrastructure finance in Haussmann's Paris. The case captures many of the key recurring issues, from land acquisition rules to financing strategies and from inventive public-private partnerships to off-budget manipulation designed to avoid fiscal limits.

The public sector's ability to use land acquisition and resale as an infrastructure financing tool depends on (a) its ability to "buy low and sell high"—

Land Finance and the Reconstruction of Paris

Baron Haussmann's reconstruction of Paris was one of the largest urban redevelopment programs ever undertaken. Although the effort is best known for its impact on urban design and architecture, it also involved massive investment in infrastructure. The new avenues and boulevards that were built came fully equipped with water and sewer lines, drainage, and utilities. A new aqueduct system brought clean water into the city, including one aqueduct that eventually delivered water from sources 600 kilometers distant.

Financing strategy. The state financed one-third of the costs of reconstruction through grants. The remaining costs were borne by the municipal government, via budgetary contributions, land sales, and borrowing. Land sales were critical to the financing strategy. Haussmann acquired huge swaths of land through condemnation and expropriation at current-use value or less. In all, more than 20,000 buildings and a large part of the Ile de la Cité were demolished to clear the way for public works and new buildings. Excess land adjoining the new avenues was sold to private promoters, after works were completed, at prices enhanced greatly by public investment. Land retained by the municipality indirectly backed the borrowing used to finance construction. The financing strategy also identified the *octroi*—a tax on goods entering the city—as the most buoyant source of current revenue that would help to repay debt. Its revenues were expected to boom as the materials needed for rebuilding were imported into the city.

Legal underpinnings. The land transactions central to financing were made possible by a decree issued in 1852, just before Haussmann assumed his role as prefect of Paris. The decree changed the rules for land expropriation. Previously, only the specific land to be used for public works could be expropriated by public action. The new decree stated that "for purposes of public interest" public authorities could acquire all the buildings and other property along avenues to be constructed. This "excess" land was able to capture for the city the land-value gains resulting from public investment. The eventual unraveling of Haussmann's financing strategy resulted from courts' later rulings, starting in the 1860s, in favor of landowners, holding that (a) landowners were entitled to higher compensation for land expropriated than had been granted by the city and that (b) excess land held by the city, but not used for actual public works, had to be returned to the original owners at the acquisition price rather than at current market value as enhanced by public investment.

(continued)

Land Finance and the Reconstruction of Paris *(continued)*

Public-private partnership and borrowing. The entire enterprise involved a new form of public-private partnership. The reconstruction project was devised and organized in detail by the state. However, private entrepreneurs carried out the investments in public as well as private facilities. They were financed off budget by a newly created municipal public works fund (*caisse de travaux*). The *caisse de travaux* was originally established as a fund to smooth over cash flows during the long period required to build infrastructure. However, it soon became a source of direct debt financing for private contractors on behalf of the city, periodically augmented by the proceeds of land sales.

Off-budget financing. The *caisse de travaux* was operated off budget and without public oversight. Haussmann was able to make financial arrangements on his own. At times, off-budget annual investment expenditures via the public works fund were more than twice total expenditures under the city's formal public budget. Haussmann also arranged other off-budget forms of borrowing to avoid council review and fiscal limits. David Harvey writes that in 1869, shortly before Haussmann resigned and the *caisse de travaux* was terminated, total outstanding debt incurred for public works stood at F2.5 billion, or 44 times the annual on-budget expenditure of the city in 1851, the year before construction started. Resentment of Haussmann's handling of financial affairs is said to have influenced the courts' decisions in favor of landowner compensation.

Sources: Pinkney (1957); Massa-Gille (1973); Marchand (1993); and Harvey (2003).

that is, to acquire land at its current-use value or at administrative prices set below market value and to sell land at full market value as enhanced by public investment, (b) its ability to buy on these terms more land than is needed for actual public works, and (c) the existence of rules that dedicate a significant portion of public land profits to infrastructure investment. Political, legal, and bureaucratic disputes over each of these elements are found wherever public land has been acquired and resold on a large scale. The story of land financing of this type is the story of public-private interaction—sometimes in partnership, sometimes in conflict.

Developer Exactions and Impact Fees

Developer exactions and impact fees, unlike value capture, approach land financing from the cost side. They are one-time, up-front charges designed to recover the infrastructure costs associated with growth. Although the terms are not distinguished consistently, developer exactions here refer to the requirement that developers either install at their own expense the internal infrastructure required to meet development standards or pay for infrastructure elements provided by public authorities. Impact fees are designed to cover the costs of the *external* infrastructure caused by new development. Growth generates demand for systemwide expansions in infrastructure capacity for roads, water supply, wastewater removal, parks, and other facilities. Impact fees and developer exactions are designed to make growth "pay its way" by requiring developers to pay for the expansion in infrastructure capacity that growth necessitates.

Developer exactions for internal infrastructure are now standard throughout most developed countries, although often they recover only part of the infrastructure costs.[2] Impact fees covering external infrastructure are limited primarily to the United States, where they have become an important part of the overall urban infrastructure financing picture. They first became popular in the 1970s in response to the tax revolt against rapidly rising local property taxes. The opposition to property taxes eventually succeeded in capping property tax rates for existing homeowners in many states, forcing authorities to find other ways to pay for the infrastructure investments required by growth. Impact fees were first introduced in states with high rates of urban expansion and voter resistance to property taxes, like Arizona, California, and Florida (see Bowles and Nelson 2007 for a recent review of the use of impact fees in the United States and their political and legal background).

The initial versions of impact fees were challenged by developers in courts. From the various court cases, basic rules have emerged about the standards that impact fees must meet to withstand legal scrutiny. These include the following:

- There must be a "rational nexus" between the impact fee charged to developers and the capital expenditure it finances. That is, the government must demonstrate that investment is required to provide services to a growing population, not merely to upgrade services provided to existing residents.

---

[2] In the United Kingdom, section 106 payments and in-kind contributions are negotiated between developers and towns for new development areas. It is estimated that, on average, these cover one-third of total infrastructure costs. See United Kingdom, Her Majesty's Treasury (2006).

- Impact fees must be limited to a "proportionate share" of infrastructure costs. The costs of infrastructure expansion that benefit both existing and new residents must be shared between tax and revenue sources so that new developments are charged, via impact fees, only their proportionate share of the costs, as measured by usage or benefits.
- All revenues from impact fees must be used exclusively for the capital investment purpose cited to justify the fee. They cannot be used to finance other parts of the local capital budget or to contribute to the operating budget.
- States must expressly authorize local governments to impose impact fees, and local governments must follow the procedures specified in the state's authorizing legislation. As of late 2006, 26 states had passed authorizing legislation, including all of the rapidly growing states.

Well-designed impact fee systems now analyze carefully the actual incremental capital costs caused by different types and sizes of development at different locations. Cost calculations are differentiated for each type of infrastructure. Impact fees are differentiated by residential, commercial, and industrial use, by house and lot size as proxies for water and wastewater demand and automobile trips, and by location relative to existing infrastructure systems and their unused capacity. The result is a highly differentiated matrix of impact fees that helps to steer development to locations where it can be accommodated most efficiently. Brueckner has demonstrated that financing growth-related infrastructure through impact fees is more economically efficient, as measured by total urban land value, than financing growth through a general property tax or other measures that spread costs over both the existing population and new development (Brueckner 1997, 2001).

Impact fees have become an important component of municipal infrastructure finance in growth areas of the United States. A recent survey of impact fee levels found that the average impact fee in 2006 for a standard 2,000 square foot house on a standard-size lot in communities responding to the survey was US$10,496. Impact fees for this standard dwelling exceeded US$50,000 in several California communities (Duncan Associates 2007). All revenues must be used to finance infrastructure requirements.

Developers' resistance to impact fees has diminished as the practice has become more standardized. The impact fee system replaces case-by-case negotiation between municipalities and developers over the financial "contributions" they must make to obtain approval to develop an area. They also provide clear rules that reduce uncertainty and delay, while ensuring that payments are used for infrastructure provision. Phoenix, Arizona, is representative of the new generation of impact fees that differentiates fee levels according to a careful analytical underpinning (see box 2.4). Phoenix's impact fee sys-

Impact Fee System in Phoenix, Arizona

Phoenix is required by state law to prepare a long-term infrastructure investment plan as the basis for its impact fees. It conducts analyses of the impacts of additional usage and costs caused by growth at different locations. Cost estimates are made separately for nine types of infrastructure and public open space, taking into account such factors as type of land use, building and lot size, water meter size, distance from infrastructure trunk lines, and other locational features. Phoenix is restricted by law to imposing impact fees only for infrastructure that must be built within the same planning district as a subdivision. A recent modification of the law requires that the incremental cost estimates be conducted by independent, third-party experts and that the methodology and results be published for public review.

The result of this analysis is a highly differentiated matrix of impact fees. Many parts of the urban area are exempted from impact fees, on the grounds that the incremental capital costs caused by growth are modest. Impact fees are concentrated on what are planned to be the fastest-growing areas, north and south of the city. The largest impact fees are for roads, water, parks, and sewer lines, in that order. The impact fee, as in other cities, must be paid at the time a construction permit is issued. Total impact fees per equivalent dwelling unit (EDU), a standardized measure that converts different types and sizes of buildings into a standardized residential equivalent, range from US$11,349 to US$31,622, depending on the location of the planning district.

Phoenix's impact fee system specifically charges new growth for a proportionate share of major repairs to existing facilities that serve new subdivisions. State law prohibits the imposition of impact fees to finance school construction, as do laws in all but eight states. Where school impact fees are permitted, as in California, they typically are the largest component of the total fee.

The significance of impact fees for local capital spending can be judged from Phoenix's investment planning. The infrastructure investment plan estimates that 336,000 equivalent dwelling units will be built over the next 25 years within the current impact fee districts. At an average impact fee of about $25,000 per EDU, impact fees in these districts will yield a total of some US$8.4 billion over the period, all of which must be invested in growth-related infrastructure. Receipts are expected to fluctuate dramatically in the short run, as a result of the boom and bust cycle in new housing.

Source: City of Phoenix, Arizona (2006).

tem is less aggressive than that found in many other high-growth cities, in that it recovers only the costs of incremental infrastructure required within a particular planning district, not the costs of citywide expansions of trunk capacity.

A well-designed impact fee system requires a strong analytical base, as well as a long-term infrastructure investment plan, to differentiate accurately the impact of new development on infrastructure costs by location, land use, lot, and building size. The technical demands are likely to strain the planning capacity of municipal governments in developing countries. An impact fee system that bypasses this kind of differentiation can be a good revenue producer, but it runs the risk of becoming a mere revenue-raising device, one that skirts property tax limits and shifts infrastructure costs to new residents (see Altschuler and Gómez-Ibáñez 1993). Courts in the United States have established the broad rules of "rational nexus" and "proportionate cost sharing" to protect against fiscal exploitation of growth. However, state courts have varied widely in the type of impact fee systems they have found to meet these standards. When impact fees are applied uniformly to new housing, without differentiation by size or location, they can add significantly to the cost of affordable housing and become an instrument of fiscal exclusion of moderate-income households.

Widespread application of impact fees in developing countries is likely to require the same kind of simplification of administration that has made betterment fees feasible. Development fees have been discussed, for example, as a way of helping to finance growth infrastructure in Greater Mumbai. A development fee levied on construction permits could be differentiated broadly by development zone, so that outlying developments, which will necessitate major investment in new infrastructure to provide basic public services, would pay more than developments close to existing infrastructure that has adequate capacity.

Land Asset Management and Land Sales

The land-financing techniques considered thus far link land revenues to specific infrastructure projects that either increase land values (value capture) or are necessitated by urban land development (cost recovery through developer exactions and impact fees).

A third form of land financing involves land asset management. For a variety of historical and legal reasons, public authorities frequently have valuable landholdings on the asset side of their balance sheets. Often, these land parcels are not being used or are not being used efficiently. Strategic asset management involves inventorying public assets and making economic decisions as to how to extract maximum value from them, including land and developed property. Often, a strategic assessment of this kind reveals that municipalities or other public agencies are overloaded with land and property assets; at the same time, they face acute infrastructure shortages. It then becomes reasonable to consider selling or leasing publicly held land in order to raise revenues to finance additional infrastructure investment (Peterson 2006).

From the perspective of the capital budget, shown in table 1.1, land sales represent a special form of capital revenue, which can be used to help finance general capital expenditures. From the perspective of the *balance sheet* of a municipality or special public authority, the net effect of selling land and investing in infrastructure is a portfolio adjustment that changes the composition of public assets. Publicly owned land is exchanged for public infrastructure. A transaction of this kind may be motivated in equal parts by the desire to increase infrastructure investment and by the conviction that land and property development can be implemented more effectively by the private sector.

Table 2.1 shows the composition of the asset side of the balance sheet of Dallas, Texas. As in most U.S. municipalities, land constitutes a relatively modest part of the municipal government's assets. Most of this land lies under public infrastructure and public buildings or is devoted to public open space. Elsewhere in the world, however, municipal governments own large amounts of undeveloped land or even possess the property rights to all land within

Table 2.1 Composition of Municipal Assets in Dallas, Texas
(US$ millions)

Asset	Assets used for government-type activities	Assets used for business-type activities	All government assets
Land	300.0	213.8	513.8
Water rights	0	283.8	203.8
Buildings	345.7	727.7	1,073.4
Other improvements	76.5	117.9	194.4
Infrastructure	774.9	278.6	1,053.5
Equipment and artwork	162.2	198.6	360.8
Utility property	0	1,113.2	1,113.2
Construction in progress	271.9	533.0	804.9
Total	1,931.3	3,466.7	5,398.1

Source: Peterson (2006, 149).

their boundaries. This land is potentially available for sale or lease. In such cases, "land" will account for a much larger share of the assets on the municipal balance sheet and take on greater financial importance relative to current revenue. Chapter 4 shows, for example, that in Changsha, a representative provincial capital city in China, municipal land available for leasing in 2002 had an estimated net market value 14 times greater than the municipality's total revenue in that year. In Dallas, by contrast, total municipal assets were only 4.1 times annual municipal revenues, and municipally owned land was valued at only 0.38 times annual municipal revenues. In other words, in China, assets on the balance sheet, and land in particular, loom much larger in the overall municipal financial picture relative to revenues from taxes or user fees. Although China is an exceptional case, the importance of land assets relative to municipalities' recurring, own-source revenues is characteristic of much of the developing world.

Even in advanced nations, where most land is held by private property owners, municipal and state development authorities often hold valuable parcels of urban land that could be converted into infrastructure. Some of these agencies are charged specifically with infrastructure investment functions that have been neglected as a result of the emphasis on other economic development activities. Box 2.5 recounts the history of the Port Authority of New York and New Jersey and its recent return to its roots as an urban infrastructure investor rather than property developer.

Lessons for Land Asset Management

The Port Authority's experience in returning to its infrastructure roots foreshadows that of many urban development authorities in the developing world. Infrastructure investment agencies often also serve as development authorities and are the principal holders of public land in cities. Political and economic forces have combined to pressure these agencies to separate their commercial development functions from their infrastructure investment functions. In the process, they have begun divesting valuable parcels of land and developed property, using the financial proceeds to strengthen their infrastructure investment capacity. Often, as in the case of the Port Authority, the infrastructure investment responsibilities most closely intermingled with economic development involve major investments in transportation. Revenues generated by land sales therefore have been tilted toward large-scale transportation initiatives.

World Trade Center and Infrastructure Investment, Port Authority of New York and New Jersey

The tragic events of September 11, 2001, have overshadowed the development history of Manhattan's World Trade Center. However, the World Trade Center is a landmark illustration of critical land development by an infrastructure agency, which extracted profits from the sale of property to reinforce its primary mission of urban infrastructure investment. The following table summarizes the project.

Summary of World Trade Center Project in New York

Executing authority	Port Authority of New York and New Jersey
Scope of project	Developed 16 acres of land in lower Manhattan into the World Trade Center, consisting of seven office buildings containing 1.24 million square meters of office space
Sale agreement and proceeds	Sold to Silverstein Properties in 2001 in the form of a 99-year lease, for a present value of US$3.2 billion
Use of funds	To finance urban transportation projects throughout the New York metropolitan area. Sale proceeds of US$3.2 billion compare to US$1.3 billion of total infrastructure capital spending by the Port Authority in 2005 and total infrastructure assets held at year-end 2004 of US$12 billion

Source: Author.

Project background. The Port Authority of New York and New Jersey was created in 1921. It was the first interstate government agency created in the United States, established under the constitutional powers granted to the states to create interstate compacts. Interstate cooperation was necessary to plan and implement development of New York harbor, which is bounded by the two states of New York and New Jersey. The Port Authority covers a regional territory of approximately 1,500 square miles, defined as a radius of 25 miles from the Statue of Liberty.

(continued)

World Trade Center and Infrastructure Investment, Port Authority of New York and New Jersey *(continued)*

Over the years, the Port Authority's responsibilities for owning and managing transportation facilities in the New York metropolitan region expanded greatly. In the 1930s, the Port Authority took over the recently built Holland Tunnel, the first interstate connection between New Jersey and Manhattan, and built the George Washington Bridge, Lincoln Tunnel, and other connectors. In the 1940s, the Port Authority took over ownership and operation of the region's principal airports, including what is now John F. Kennedy International Airport, LaGuardia Airport, and Newark International Airport. Facilities at the airports were expanded and modernized to accommodate world trade.

In the 1950s and 1960s, the Port Authority built the Port Authority Bus Terminal in Manhattan, the largest bus terminal in the United States, constructed a second deck to the George Washington Bridge, built the world's first containership ports at Newark and Elizabeth, New Jersey, and established the PATH commuter rail system, which now carries 71 million people annually from New Jersey to Manhattan.

The Port Authority is a self-financing infrastructure agency. It has no taxing powers and receives no dedicated tax revenues. It does not receive operating subsidies from state government. It finances itself through fees and charges levied on users of transportation services and rents charged to commercial and retail occupants at airports. Historically, the Port Authority has received only small capital contributions from New York and New Jersey for specific capital projects and occasional capital grants from the federal government. It has consistently generated a positive net revenue stream, which it has borrowed against to finance its capital investment. At the end of fiscal 2006, the Port Authority had US$9.1 billion of bonds and other long-term debt outstanding, backed by its operating revenue stream, without state guarantees or tax support.

Development project history. During the 1970s, the Port Authority turned to the World Trade Center as its primary investment program. The Port Authority's mission always had called for it to manage transportation infrastructure for the benefit of economic development of the region. In the 1970s and 1980s, economic development became the principal investment objective. The development goal behind the World Trade Center was to revitalize lower

(continued)

World Trade Center and Infrastructure Investment, Port Authority of New York and New Jersey *(continued)*

Manhattan, which had lagged behind the midtown area in development as a financial center. The Port Authority also invested in a variety of other development projects, including the Teleport, special industrial development zones, and major commercial and retail projects.

Construction of the World Trade Center was carried out over more than a decade, primarily on land previously occupied by the terminal of a bankrupt railroad. The Port Authority built seven large commercial office buildings on the site, including the iconic Twin Towers, the tallest buildings in New York City, at a total investment cost (including infrastructure) of US$900 million. In early 2001 the World Trade Center accounted for roughly 4 percent of all the office space in Manhattan.

In 1998, the decision was made to privatize the World Trade Center in order to focus the Port Authority's management and capital investment program on core transportation infrastructure, much of which had significantly deteriorated due to lack of repair and reinvestment. After vigorous competitive bidding, a contract was signed with Silverstein Properties involving a 99-year lease for US$3.2 billion. The final contract documents were signed in July 2001, just seven weeks before the attack that destroyed all of the World Trade Center. This case study examines the property sale as it was intended to take effect, absent the 9/11 tragedy.

Institutional context and evolution leading to property sale. The decision to sell the World Trade Center was the direct result of pressure for the Port Authority to return its focus to transportation infrastructure. As stated in the Port Authority's long-range capital plan, prepared in 2005, and in its recent annual reports, the priorities now are to "return the agency to its roots: making landmark investments in transportation infrastructure [and] meeting commitments to rebuild and improve facilities." The updated 10-year capital plan for the period 2007–16 reflects these priorities. Total investment over the decade by the Port Authority is projected at US$29.55 billion. Less than 0.5 percent of this amount is targeted for economic development. Most is targeted either for a program—State of Good Repair—intended to keep existing infrastructure facilities in good operating and capital condition or for specific new infrastructure projects, such as new tunnel access to Manhattan, airport expansion, and seaport modernization via ship-to-rail connections.

(continued)

World Trade Center and Infrastructure Investment, Port Authority of New York and New Jersey *(continued)*

Returning the focus of the Port Authority to transportation investment was very much a result of political pressure. Divestment of the World Trade Center was at the core of this effort. During the mid-1990s, the governors of both New York and New Jersey pushed for the Port Authority to narrow its mission. At the time the sale of the World Trade Center was announced, Governor Pataki of New York issued a statement, saying, in part, "From my first day in office, I have pushed hard to privatize the management and operation of the World Trade Center because I believe government is at its best when it focuses on its core mission … By sharpening the agency's focus on our airports, seaports, bridges, and tunnels, the Port Authority can become a stronger economic engine for the entire region." Despite the 9/11 tragedy, the Port Authority has successfully moved forward with its refocused plan for investment in transportation infrastructure.

Sources: Doig (2001); Port Authority of New York and New Jersey (2005, 2006, 2007a, 2007b).

3.

LAND-BASED INFRASTRUCTURE FINANCE IN DEVELOPING COUNTRIES

This chapter looks at the way land-based financing techniques are being used to finance infrastructure investment in developing countries. These countries face the same conceptual issues in implementing land finance as developed nations. In addition, they have their own traditions of landownership and public planning. Many have poorer cadastral systems that provide less reliable and less extensive information about the characteristics of land parcels and their market value. This has forced countries to modify the basic tools of land finance to fit local conditions.

The chapter discusses land-financing techniques in broadly the same sequence as chapter 2. It examines first the recovery of infrastructure invest-ment costs through developer land sales at the scale of new towns. It then considers the changes made to betterment levies to make them a practical instrument of infrastructure finance. The chapter's third section considers public ownership and acquisition of land as a way of capturing land-value gains caused by major infrastructure projects. Capturing land-value gains through the sale of property has been the most common but also the most controversial of land-financing instruments. In one variation, municipalities sell development rights around infrastructure projects rather than actual land. The final section looks at the practical application of developer exactions and impact fees.

The experience described here is not representative of all developing-country experience—it is more likely "leading-edge" experience—but the chapter considers the potential for generalizing each approach beyond the case study locations.

Developer Investment in Infrastructure: New Cities in Cairo, Egypt

It is common in developing countries for "urban" land to have a different landowning regime than rural or desert land. In North Africa and the Middle East desert land tends to be owned by the state, just as desert land in the state of Arizona in the United States is owned by a state land trust. Urban land and cultivated agricultural land are subject to private, freehold ownership. However, as urban areas grow under population pressures, the two landholding regimes converge. The built-up region expands onto raw land at the urban fringe. This area must be prepared for urbanization through infrastructure investment, and a process must be designed for transferring land from public ownership to private ownership.

The state landowner faces three choices. It can sell raw land to private developers and leave infrastructure installation to some combination of private initiative and municipal investment. It can finance formal development itself through public investment in both infrastructure and publicly constructed housing and then sell the finished property on the market, perhaps retaining low- and moderate-income housing in public hands for subsidized rental. Or it can install the basic infrastructure needed for urban development and sell serviced land. Many countries in North Africa and elsewhere are now pursuing the third alternative, which gives national and municipal authorities control over the location of urban expansion, while harnessing private entrepreneurship to develop the serviced land sites. In the Arab Republic of Egypt, the strategy is being implemented at the scale of new cities. The strategy represents a move toward public-private partnership in developing property for urban expansion, away from previous approaches where the state operated both as infrastructure investor and final developer.

Cairo's New Cities

The most immediately apparent difference between new towns outside of Cairo and new towns in Denmark and the United Kingdom is scale. Whereas Orestad (chapter 2) is planning to attract 60,000 workers and 30,000 residents within a decade, the new cities and new communities outside of Cairo are expected to house more than 5.6 million residents by 2015 (El Kovedia and Madbourly 2007). Two of the new cities—6th October and New Cairo—are each planned to accommodate some 2.5 million residents eventually. Twenty new cities already have been established in Egypt, and 44 additional sites have been identified for new settlement construction. In each case, the New Urban Communities Authority (NUCA) controls land covering not just the service area presently planned for development, but a 5-kilometer extension of additional land in all directions to allow for future, unplanned growth. Most of the new towns are located in the area surrounding Cairo.

Egypt's new towns policy reflects its experience with informal squatter settlements. More than 10 million residents now reside in the informally developed, unplanned, and unmapped areas outside the original central city. Most informal development has taken place on agricultural land, because agricultural land is subject to private ownership and private landowners have sold land for conversion to informal urban use. It is estimated that 300,000 acres of agricultural land around Cairo have been lost to informal urban expansion (El Kovedia and Madbourly 2007). The construction of new towns has been deemed the only way to accommodate Cairo's continued rapid growth, while establishing formal sector development standards and preserving agricultural land (Salheen 2006). Under Egyptian law, the desert land where new cities and new communities are being built belongs to the state, which by decree of the prime minister has transferred the land for new settlements to NUCA. A 100-meter margin on both sides of access highways built to connect the new cities to Cairo also has been ceded, free of charge, to NUCA.

The infrastructure investment requirements for land development on this scale are massive. Through 2005, NUCA had provided infrastructure services to 435 square kilometers of land in new communities, at an estimated cost (in today's currency) of £E160 per square meter, or a total cost of some £E 69.6 billion (US$12.7 billion; World Bank 2006, vol. 2). These are costs of internal infrastructure. The costs of connecting internal infrastructure systems to major trunk lines for highways, electricity, telecommunications, and water supply are estimated to be even higher.

Egypt has addressed the costs of development through an evolving policy of public-private collaboration. The standard practice has been for the public sector to install both internal and external infrastructure, at public expense, and to allocate land to private promoters through private negotiations or sales at prefixed, below-market prices for investment in housing, commercial, and industrial facilities. From a financial perspective, this arrangement has placed heavy burdens on the public budget. From an urban development perspective, it has failed to take advantage of the efficiency of market price signals. Development has been driven by public decisions about where to install infrastructure, but often infrastructure has been installed where there was no user demand for housing or economic activity. New cities have lagged behind their expected growth, in part because infrastructure investment has been targeted at distant locations, unrelated to market demand (World Bank 2006, vol. 1).

The financial loss from selling land through private negotiation or administratively assigned prices can be gauged from two illustrations. In 2004, it was decided to open to public auction a substantial land parcel (378,000 square meters) at the main entrance to one of the new cities, New Cairo. At that time the administrative price set for sale of publicly owned land in all of New Cairo, regardless of the parcel's location within the city, was £E 225 per square meter, barely enough to cover the costs incurred in providing internal infrastructure. Four developers participated in the competitive auction, at a winning price of £E 625 (about US$114) per square meter, or almost triple the administrative price. From an aggregate perspective, the land sale policy in effect until 2005 failed to recover even the costs of internal infrastructure investment. In the last 25 years Egypt has recovered from land sales in new communities less than half the amount it has invested in internal infrastructure alone.

Auction Reforms

Recently initiated reforms have begun to overhaul the way NUCA (and the Ministry of Housing, Utilities, and Urban Development that oversees it) does business. The reforms can be summed up in two phrases: land auctions and public-private participation in infrastructure investment. Both policy changes place land financing at the center of new town infrastructure development.

Government's announced policy now is to sell at public auction all substantial land parcels in new cities and new communities that are designated for middle- or upper-income housing, retail, or commercial development. Land is being auctioned off in response to developers' expressed interest in particular sites, reflective of market demand, as well as government planning priorities.

The first fruits of this policy were witnessed in May 2007, when several land parcels in new city areas were sold for a total of US$3.12 billion. This was the first auction to take full advantage of international competitive bidding and was part of a government asset management initiative that involved the privatization of a variety of other government-held assets (see chapter 4 for further discussion). Government announced that proceeds from the land sale, which substantially exceeded the costs of installing internal infrastructure, would be used to pay for a new four-lane access highway that connected to the Cairo Ring Road and for subsidies to provide low-income housing within the new city development areas. Additional large land areas are scheduled for future sale at auction.

The new pricing and auction policy improves the prospects that the public sector will be able to recover the entire infrastructure costs associated with new cities, internal and external, as long as demand for urbanization continues at the rate projected.

Public-Private Partnership for Infrastructure Installation
The second major reform involves the approach to infrastructure provision in the new cities. Traditionally, NUCA installed all local infrastructure prior to land sales. A new experiment has reversed this policy, giving private developers greater responsibility for infrastructure investment. At the same time it has reversed the roles that the public and private sectors play in land readjustment schemes as traditionally applied in Japan, the Republic of Korea, and elsewhere. In traditional land readjustment, private owners are the original landowners. They hand over control of their land to public authorities for infrastructure investment and preparation for urban development. At the end of the process, the private landowners receive back a portion of the developed land—say, 40 percent. In this arrangement, private owners provide the land, public authorities provide the infrastructure and planning authorizations for urban development, and, at the end of the process, private owners receive back a portion of their original land, greatly enhanced in value by infrastructure investment and planning authorization. The public sector uses the remaining portions of land for roads, public buildings, open space, and other public uses.

In Cairo's variant of this arrangement, the public sector (NUCA) provides the land, transferring it to private ownership, while the developer installs the infrastructure. The private developer is expected to accelerate infrastructure installation in his own interest. The public sector benefits by having infrastructure installed without financial costs as well as by gaining a portion of serviced land for public use. The developer meanwhile retains the bulk of land, having paid only for the installation of infrastructure. This arrangement is being pursued in several locations. In the largest-scale application, the private developer is providing not only internal infrastructure but a significant portion of external infrastructure as well (see box 3.1). The agreement commits the private developer to invest more than US$1 billion in what traditionally has been "public" infrastructure.

Potential for Application Elsewhere
Significant public landholdings are a distinguishing characteristic of North African and Middle Eastern countries. In these countries, as in Egypt, the state typically owns the desert land available for urban expansion. Allocation of this land has been problematic, characterized by bureaucratic procedures that ignore market incentives and fail to recover the costs of public investment. Government control has been justified by the need to subsidize land allocations for low-income housing development. However, sale of land for middle-class and upper-class uses at full market value, coupled with transparent cross-subsidization of low-income housing from land profits, seems

Madinaty: Infrastructure Development through Public-Private Partnership in New Cairo, Egypt

Within New Cairo, a mega real estate project, Madinaty, is under implementation, representing the largest real estate development project ever built in Egypt, extending over an area of 3,360 hectares. The project is being implemented by the Alexandria Company for Urban Development. After negotiations, the New Urban Communities Authority agreed to supply the developer with free land, in return for the developer's provision of basic infrastructure. The private company will install internal infrastructure valued at £E 110 per square meter and some external infrastructure (including connections to the electrical and telecommunication grids) valued at £E 127 per square meter. The partnership arrangement leaves NUCA responsible only for external connections covering water supply, sewerage, and roads. As part of the deal, the investment company also will supply NUCA with housing for low-income households, equal to 7 percent of total development costs.

Source: World Bank (2006, vol. 2, 60).

to be a more effective means of meeting social needs than government land allocations that defy the market.

Several countries in the region have potential for adapting Egypt's experience (information in this paragraph is drawn from Wahba 2007). Tunisia, for example, now sells land serviced with infrastructure and approved for new development via a specialized government agency. Its policy is to recover the costs of internal infrastructure installation, which results in land prices that are about 50 percent of market value. This is one of the more market-oriented land disposition policies. However, if land for middle- and upper-income housing as well as land for commercial and retail uses were sold at full market value, the proceeds would provide a margin for cross-subsidization of low-income housing development and financing of major external infrastructure links. In Morocco, the supply of state-owned land for development has lagged far behind market demand, leading to a royal order to release 8,000 hectares of land for housing under the Cities Without Slums Program. In Saudi Arabia and the Republic of Yemen, the government provides free land to households or sells it at a fraction of market value. This has led to backlogs in infrastructure coverage as well as rampant land speculation. Tunisia and Morocco, like the Islamic Republic of Iran, Kuwait, Saudi Arabia, and the Republic of Yemen, are just beginning to integrate market forces into urban land supply.

Betterment Levies: Bogotá and Cali, Colombia

Colombia long has been cited for its successful use of contribución de valorización, a form of betterment levy, to finance urban infrastructure. In reality, however, Colombia has wrestled with the same problems of implementation that have plagued developed countries, as reviewed in chapter 2. The scheme was expensive to implement and led to countless disputes over the land-value gains assigned as the basis for the levy.

Valorización as previously administered in Colombia combined elements of both benefit capitalization and cost recovery. The law, although applicable for a wide variety of public works, in practice was applied mostly to road construction and road improvements. It allocated payments from landowners proportionately to the estimated increase in land values resulting from public works (benefit capitalization). However, the total amount to be collected was based on cost recovery, defined as the following:

- 100 percent of (budgeted) infrastructure costs plus
- 10 percent contingency fee plus
- 30 percent administrative costs.

Land-value gains were not measured by market prices or appraisals; rather they were estimated beforehand through a formula based on various factors, including size of the land parcel, location relative to the infrastructure work, land-use activity, and others. Revenue was collected before and during project construction and was not adjusted ex post for actual changes in land prices.

Valorización implemented in this form had several difficulties. The a priori formulas used to estimate land-value gains from public investment often produced results at odds with actual market values, leading to a series of legal challenges. The system required that the total betterment levy recover 140 percent of estimated infrastructure costs, whether or not land-value gains were of this magnitude. The 30 percent additional charge for administrative costs called attention to the administrative inefficiency of the system.

These defects had consequences for the way valorización was used in practice (information in this paragraph is drawn largely from Jaramillo 2001). First, to minimize protests by landowners, public authorities substantially underestimated the costs of infrastructure projects when they applied the law. This action lessened the burden on levy payers, but underfunded infrastructure investment. Second, public authorities tended to use the betterment levy only in wealthier areas, where landowners had the capacity to pay. This had the effect of also focusing infrastructure improvements on wealthier areas. Finally, and most noticeably, cities' use of valorización declined dramatically over time. Between 1968 and 1978, municipal revenue from valorización declined by almost 50 percent in real terms; between 1980 and 1990, municipal revenue from valorización fell from 15 percent of total municipal revenues to 5 percent. As shown in table 3.1, the importance of the betterment levy as a source of revenue in Bogotá and Cali fell even more precipitously.

In recognition of the difficulties of implementing valorización, the government in 1997 changed the law in fundamental respects. The more innovative and more publicized of the changes introduced the principle of levying a betterment charge on urban planning authorizations. Land parcels within a special planning district, where the municipal government had authorized conversion of land from rural to urban use or rezoned land for higher density, could be subjected to a betterment levy of 30 to 50 percent, at municipal discretion. The betterment levy was applied to the price increment enjoyed by the landowner as a result of planning authorization. Payment of the betterment levy was due on realization of the land-value gain at the time of land sale or development. Proceeds are to be used for infrastructure investment to support the newly urbanized territory.

At the same time, the law was changed to make implementation of traditional valorización more flexible. Municipalities now have discretion over the percentage of infrastructure costs that will be recovered through valorización. The automatic add-on for administrative costs and contingencies has been eliminated.

Table 3.1 Share of Valorización in Municipal Revenues in Bogotá and Cali, Colombia, 1980–90

(percent)

Year	Bogotá	Cali
1980	5.1	31.7
1983	13.5	18.0
1990	1.4	8.9

Source: Jaramillo (2001).

Bogotá's Use of Valorización

Bogotá has been very active in using the new version of valorización. Bogotá's practical innovation has been to spread valorización over an entire package of road and other upgrading projects, distributed around the entire city. In the period 1997–2007, it financed through valorización 217 public works projects (mostly street, bridge, and drainage improvements) in all parts of the city (Rojas Rojas 2007; Saldies Barrenocha 2007). In conjunction with this action it has introduced additional factors into calculation of the betterment levy. In addition to six types of land use, graded so that betterment levies fall more heavily on commercial-industrial uses than on residential use, there are factors that take into account community income level and ability to pay, as well as the traditional factors of parcel size and location relative to public works improvements.

The result of these modifications is a less pure version of value capture. Betterment levies are no longer tied specifically to increments in land value and have abandoned the principle of assessing land values according to the highest and best economic use for a site, in favor of reductions in valuations for low- and moderate-income housing and other current uses. Valorización in effect has been transformed into an up-front, land-based infrastructure tax, used to finance a substantial part of the municipal capital budget. Over the decade 1997–2007, more than US$1 billion of municipal public works were financed in this manner. The exact formula that the city uses to assign betterment levies is virtually impenetrable, but, since it does not purport to be based on actual gains in land values, it is much more difficult to challenge in court. The fact that public works improvements financed by the betterment levy have been spread over the entire city has reduced public resistance. Bogotá also has allowed citizens to pay the betterment levy over a five-year period, if they choose. This has reduced the economic burden on property owners and allowed valorización payments to be used to repay short-term borrowing undertaken to finance construction.

The manner in which valorización fits into an overall infrastructure financing strategy is illustrated by a new program launched by Bogotá's mayor in late 2007. The program calls for citywide improvement of streets and related infrastructure. In its first phase, it will finance 188 public works projects and raise about US$350 million in valorización revenues. The mayor announced that 1,236,346 landowners will pay the valorización, based on the formula described above. Revenues from the betterment levy are embedded in a broader financing strategy that includes a US$50 million loan from the International Finance Corporation (IFC), a US$50 million loan from the Andean

Development Corporation (ADC), and a US$300 million international, peso-linked bond issue (IFC 2008; for further perspective on Bogotá's capital financing, see RTI International 2005). Both the IFC loan and the ADC loan are targeted expressly to street improvements, while the bond issue is available to finance other public investments as well. Within this strategy, valorización pays roughly half of the total cost of street and bridge improvements. The mayor has announced that between 2008 and 2015, successive stages of valorización will raise Col$2.1 trillion (US$1.1 billion) to finance citywide infrastructure improvements.

Potential for Application Elsewhere

Bogotá's experience is being replicated elsewhere in Colombia. Use of valorización has been revived in Medellín and Barranquilla. Cali's mayor is now attempting to copy Bogotá's experience, and, if successful, the strategy can be expected to spread further within Colombia. Cali's proposal, announced in February 2008, is summarized in box 3.2.

Application beyond Colombia also is possible. Most Latin American countries have had betterment laws like the contribución de valorización or contribución por mejoras in the past, including Argentina, Brazil, Chile, Ecuador, Honduras, Mexico, Panama, Peru, and the República Boliviana de Venezuela, among others. Many of these laws remain on the books. They once financed a significant part of local public works improvements, but have declined in importance for the same reasons they have declined elsewhere.[1] A series of recent regional conferences has monitored revival of valorización in Colombia and examined the possibility of applying the approach in other Latin American nations that draw on the same Spanish legal tradition.

Value Capture via Land Sale for Major Projects: China and India

The most common strategy for recovering infrastructure costs involves the sale of land whose value has been enhanced by infrastructure investment or zoning changes. If the public sector owns the land, it can internalize the benefits of public investment and capture the gains through land sale. The potential for land gain also opens the way for different types of public-private partnerships, in which the public sector contributes land, while the private sector partner builds and finances the infrastructure.

In countries where most land is owned by private landowners, the public sector must first acquire the land. If it can acquire excess land, beyond that

---

[1] Ecuador has a law that allows municipalities to impose betterment levies at a progressive rate up to 42 percent of land-value gain, but municipalities have not used the law. Peru has a law allowing municipalities to levy rates between 20 and 50 percent on land-value gains, at their discretion, but the law has not been used since 1993. See Furtado and Jorgenson (2006).

Proposed Valorización Program in Cali, Colombia

Cali turned to valorización as a consequence of a drastically declining capital budget and parallel deterioration in the condition of infrastructure. The program is aimed at road and bridge repairs, with a small element of new road construction. In 2007, Cali's capital spending on roads fell to about US$15 million. Capital expenditure has been constrained by the city's debt condition. In the 1990s, Colombia devolved gasoline taxes to the local level to support road construction and repair. Most cities in the country borrowed heavily against the new revenue stream. As the country fell into fiscal straits, and local governments defaulted on their loans, workouts were arranged that intercepted most of the local gas tax for debt repayment. In Cali's case, 70 percent of the city's gas tax receipts are pledged for the next 10 years to support debt repayment.

The mayor's proposal calls for a vast increase in road investment—a multiyear program encompassing some US$240 million in road and bridge improvements. The program is to be financed primarily by valorización, defined in a manner similar to Bogotá's program. A package of road improvements will be spread throughout the city, and valorización will be based on a complex (yet to be fully disclosed) formula that assigns betterment levies to individual properties based on a combination of land value, land size, distance from public works improvements, land use, and proxies for community and individual income level.

The mayor summarized the program as follows: "What we want to do is benefit the people that pay the contribution. We want to valorizar the city. We plan to do it by using a general valorización, so that the works benefit the entire city and the entire city pays." In this variant of land financing, the valorización loses its strict relationship to land-value increments and becomes a generalized benefit levy, tied broadly to land-value gains. The burden of the proposed levy is tilted toward empty lots, which it is said will account for 25 to 45 percent of the total receipts. Cali also has followed Bogotá's example in allowing citizens to pay over five years if necessary. Public and political reaction to the mayor's proposal has been mixed.

Source: A series of articles in the January and February 2008 issues of *El País,* Cali's newspaper.

required for infrastructure construction, it has the potential to capture land-value gains created by infrastructure investment. Profitable acquisition and sale of land have been somewhat easier in developing countries than in the West because of the rules regarding land acquisition by public authorities. In Western Europe and the United States, public authorities that wish to acquire land for public purposes now must do so through eminent domain, subject to well-defined legal restrictions. Land generally must be purchased at market value, including the market's valuation of the future benefits to flow from planned infrastructure projects. If the public buyer and private seller cannot agree on fair compensation, the legal system prescribes specific steps for resolving disputes and establishing fair market value. Except for urban redevelopment projects, public authorities generally are prohibited from using eminent domain to acquire more land than is needed for actual infrastructure construction. They cannot use the powers of compulsory acquisition to obtain additional surrounding land that they can later sell for a profit.

In the developing world, the rules governing public acquisition of land are more variable and, often, more flexible. The public sector may already own the land in question, so its acquisition by an infrastructure financing body is a matter of government transfer rather than open-market purchase. Legal rules may empower municipalities and public authorities to acquire private land at current-use value, at administratively set prices, or may leave the determination of price up to a negotiation that favors the public sector. The set of rules is similar to that found in many Western countries in the nineteenth century, when urban growth was at its peak. The legal setting has made it possible for public agencies to be more aggressive in acquiring land and internalizing value gains from public investment. However, it also has generated controversy and political resistance over how much power government should have to capture land profits in this way.

Urban Highway Construction in China

Urban highway construction in China illustrates maximum leveraging of land values into infrastructure. In China, all urban land is owned by the municipal government. The potential for land-value gains has been central to financing urban infrastructure projects, both directly and through public-private partnerships. The process can be illustrated by the construction of the outer Ring Road encircling the region around Changsha, the capital of Hunan Province in central China. The total cost of the six-lane highway was projected in 2001 at Y6 billion, then about US$730 million. To build the highway, the municipality turned to the Ring Road Corporation, a public-private joint venture company listed on the Shanghai Stock Exchange, but majority controlled by the Hunan provincial government (Peterson 2007).

Changsha financed the highway at no out-of-pocket cost. Instead, it transferred to the Ring Road Corporation land-use and development rights for strips of land 200 meters wide on both sides of the circumferential highway that was to be built. In all, 33 square kilometers of land were transferred, or 3,300 hectares. Of this total, approximately 12 square kilometers were finished land, possessing infrastructure access and development approvals. In its original state, without access to roads or development approvals, the remaining land had very little market value. However, the plan was to sell off parcels of land once the highway was built.

Approximately half of the total highway cost was financed up front by the sale of leasing rights to the land with infrastructure service. The other half was initially financed through borrowing. The Ring Road Corporation was able to borrow from the China Development Bank and commercial banks some US$350 million against the *future* anticipated value of the improved land, pledging to repay the loans from revenues that would be received when land parcels were leased, after highway construction was completed. Municipal governments in China are prohibited from direct borrowing. However, as is often the case, the municipal government in this instance provided banks with a "comfort letter" stating that it would take steps to ensure that the Ring Road Corporation could repay its debt. The arrangement underlying the comfort letter was an understanding that the municipal government would transfer to the Ring Road Corporation additional land, suitable for immediate development and leasing, in the event that there was a revenue shortfall in meeting debt service.

In Changsha's case, as in many others, land financing was combined with toll charges to form an overall financing strategy. Major bridges on the Ring Road were built by the same joint venture and financed with cost recovery through tolls. In the end, the highway was built and financed as planned.

An entire generation of urban highways and other urban public works has been financed throughout China by direct municipal land leasing combined with borrowing against land collateral. However, the risks inherent in this model are clear. Municipally owned land has become the principal collateral for municipal-level borrowing. Although the law prohibits direct municipal borrowing, municipal corporations and joint ventures of different types can borrow backed by municipal comfort letters. The ultimate security for this balance sheet borrowing is the value of municipally owned land.

Borrowing that is based on *future* appreciation of land values is particularly risky, given the history of land market fluctuations in China and elsewhere. In fact, one of the first steps that the government of China took in limiting the risk of subnational debt (in 2003) was to require that banks making loans to municipalities appraise land collateral at its current market value rather than at its projected value after the completion of infrastructure facilities. As China's government also has recognized, land leasing cannot be the primary source of infrastructure finance indefinitely. As larger and larger portions of municipally owned land are leased out to private parties, the room for incremental generation of revenue from further leasing diminishes. The major cities of China's coastal region by now have largely exhausted land-leasing revenue as a source of infrastructure finance, after 15–20 years of reliance on it. They have had to switch to greater use of user fees and other project revenue streams to collateralize borrowing and recover infra-structure costs.

Nonetheless, in countries where local governments own substantial sup-plies of land, it makes sense to design infrastructure projects so that land-value gains can be captured by the public sector to help in financing or to transfer land-leasing rights to private builders of public infrastructure as pay-ment for infrastructure works. Even the use of publicly owned land to collat-eralize borrowing for infrastructure finance is appropriate, when done prudently.[2]

Urban Airport Construction in India

One of the most successful examples of public-private partnership in urban infrastructure finance involves India's airport modernization strategy. India's publicly owned airports long have been a notorious bottleneck for economic development. In 2006, the prime minister chaired a committee on infrastruc-ture that authorized a 40,000 crore (about US$10 billion; 1 crore equals Rs10 million) investment plan for modernizing India's airports. More than three-fourths of the financing amount, corresponding to airports in larger cities, would come from public-private partnerships, in which the private partners would also have responsibility for airport management. The plan calls for new greenfield airports to be built in Bangalore, Hyderabad, and five other locations as well as for modernization and expansion of existing airports in Chennai, Delhi, Kolkata, and Mumbai. The plan is on fast-track implemen-tation, with the two greenfield airports in Bangalore and Hyderabad having opened on schedule in spring of 2008. Table 3.2 summarizes the planned air-port investments.

---

[2] Mello-Roos legislation in California allows private developers of subdivisions to borrow against land values to finance installation of water, sewer, streets, and other subdivision works. As property is sold to individual buyers, a payment for debt service is added to the property tax bill (but does not count against property tax limits). In recognition of the risks involved in land valuations and project completion, the law requires land collateral that is appraised at three times the amount of debt. Despite this protection, Mello-Roos bonds are viewed as relatively high risk, given the steep fluctuations in real estate markets.

Table 3.2 Urban Airport Investment in India

Airport location	Type of project	Amount invested (crore)
Delhi and Mumbai	Modernization and expansion	11,400
Bangalore and Hyderabad	Greenfield airports	4,000
Chennai and Kolkata	Modernization and expansion	5,700
Five other greenfield airports for major cities	Greenfield airports	8,500
Other metro airports	Modernization	1,500
Total financed through public-private partnerships	All types (sum of above)	31,100
35 nonmetro airports financed by public sector	All types	9,000

Source: Secretariat of the Committee on Infrastructure (2006).
Note: 1 crore = Rs10 million = US$250,000.

Bangalore International Airport

Bangalore International Airport was one of the first greenfield airports to open under the program. It began commercial operations in April 2008. The international consortium (Bangalore International Airport Ltd, or BIAL) that built and operates the airport is led by Siemens (40 percent interest) and Unique Zurich (operator of Zurich Airport and other airports, 17 percent interest). It includes Karnataka State Industrial Investment and Development Corporation as well domestic private partners.

Land has been critical to several parts of the agreement with BIAL. The public sector had to acquire through eminent domain land for the airport itself. But modern, privately operated airports do not generate their revenues or profits only from aviation activities. They profit from hotels, restaurants, convention centers, commercial-industrial centers, upscale housing enclaves, and other uses of land surrounding the airport.[3] The ability to profit from surrounding land is particularly important to the economics of airport operations in a regulated environment like India's, because aviation activities are subject to pricing controls by the Aviation Authority, while other activities are subject only to market pricing.

In the case of Bangalore International Airport, the Karnataka Industrial Areas Development Board acquired through notification and compulsory

---

[3] The private British Airports Authority, which operates Heathrow Airport and other airports, earns 72 percent of its revenue from activity other than aviation. See KPMG (2006).

acquisition 4,260 acres for the airport and surrounding development. It contributed 3,850 acres to the airport consortium, BIAL, of which roughly 2,000 acres were required for aviation activities and the remainder was available for complementary activities or commercial development, including a 300-acre parcel along the principal access road. The BIAL consortium invested a budgeted 1,930 crore (US$490 million) in airport construction. Land was Karnataka's primary contribution (it also invested 350 crore), for which it received a 26 percent share in the BIAL consortium as well as the development benefits of a modern airport, built in 32 months at no additional out-of-pocket expense, to accommodate 9 million to 10 million passengers.

The airport was built on time and on budget. It represents a major infrastructure achievement. However, complications have arisen over the excess land acquired and retained by Karnataka. A little more than 400 acres were retained by state authorities. The initial plan was to sell this land at auction, either as a single parcel or as a package of 25-acre sites, and to use the proceeds to build an expressway connecting the airport to central Bangalore. The new airport is located 34 kilometers from Bangalore. Access via existing roads, some of which are only two lanes, takes more than two hours. As originally proposed, during the same time period that the private-led consortium was building the airport, public authorities were supposed to construct a new direct-access highway, financed by the proceeds of excess land sales. In this manner Karnataka would capture some of the land-value benefits generated by airport construction and plow the profits back into publicly financed infrastructure.

In financial terms, the project seemed more than feasible. The 400 acres of land near the airport were estimated in early 2007 to command a minimum value of 2,000 crore (about US$500 million). The planned expressway and flyovers would cost considerably less, even after taking into account the acquisition of land for rights-of-way. Through the early stages of planning, it was repeatedly stated that the expressway would be ready for use when the airport opened.

The public side of the infrastructure plan has broken down. Land has yet to be acquired for the expressway, and purchases are being held up by numerous court challenges launched by current landowners. Meanwhile, Karnataka authorities have retreated from their plan to sell airport land at auction. Instead, it appears that portions of the land (valued at a minimum of US$1.25 million per acre) will be given to government authorities for government office buildings. The Karnataka State Industrial Investment and Development Corporation has stated that it prefers to build industrial facilities at public expense and lease them to private operators, rather than sell land to private buyers.

Public complaints from farmers over the terms of land acquisition have led the state government to say that it will return an eighth of an acre of airport land to farmers for each acre of land that was originally acquired.[4]

Lessons from Bangalore's Experience

Bangalore's experience points up both the potential advantages and the risks involved in public acquisition of excess land from which it can benefit when infrastructure projects are completed. The theory behind land financing holds that the value created by public infrastructure investment is an "unearned increment" that should flow to the community, not to individual landowners. This argument earns more sympathy when landowners are wealthy owners of large tracts of land than when they are individual farmers.

Stable use of land financing of this kind requires a well-defined set of rules as to what prices public authorities must pay for compulsory acquisitions of land, how much excess land they can acquire, and the uses to which excess land can be put. A legal regime of this kind would define how the land-value gains from infrastructure projects are to be shared between landowners, infrastructure investors (public or private), and the general public budget. Table 3.3 illustrates the extreme variation in rules about the acquisition and resale of public land in select locations in Asia. Rules not only vary greatly between countries but also tend to be unstable within countries, as laws are changed or political practice moves ahead without adherence to the law.

The emergence of public-private partnerships as a vehicle for investing in major infrastructure projects may help to develop the legal framework. These partnerships are subject to specific contracts between the public and private partners. They spell out how land will be allocated, the commercial activities that will be allowed, and how prices will be determined. Such partnerships push toward maximizing economic returns. They therefore raise issues that the courts and government have to resolve in establishing the ground rules for future partnerships. The following is one example: the desire of BIAL and other greenfield airport developers to obtain as much excess land as possible and develop it for commercial use has led government to impose restrictions on the kind of auxiliary activities that can be developed on land granted as part of airport deals. In particular, the restrictions prohibit the development

---

[4] India has a land acquisition system in which the price of a piece of land is frozen as of the date that public authorities give notice that they intend to acquire it for public purpose. Given that a decade or more may pass between the date of notification and the date of actual purchase, the government is buying land at the price of a much earlier time, in a market where land prices have been rising 20–40 percent annually.

Table 3.3   Rules for the Acquisition and Resale of Public Land in Select Asian Locations

Country or city	Type of land purchase	Rules for purchase and compensation	Rules or practice for acquiring excess land	Land sale procedure and use of proceeds
China	Rules for municipal acquisition of rural land prior to 2007. In March 2007, a new property rights law was passed. It remains to be seen how it will be implemented.	Rural collectives could sell land only to municipalities; no other purchaser was allowed. Individual farmers were prohibited from selling. Only collectives could sell. Minimum compensation was fixed by law at a multiple of the last three years' income from farming (far below market value of land) plus resettlement costs. In practice, municipalities often negotiated prices that were far below market prices.	Municipalities were notorious for acquiring excess land beyond that planned for current urban use. They acquired huge amounts for industrial development zones that never materialized. Central government has cracked down on this practice and required municipalities to return land from development zones that lacked proper permits.	Municipalities are free to lease land at market rates. No legal restriction is placed on the use of land-leasing proceeds, although in practice they are used largely to finance infrastructure and development projects.
India	Rules vary somewhat by state. In Karnataka, public agencies can use compulsory acquisition of land for "public.	Compensation is based on government-identified market value at the time of notification of intended acquisition. Long periods	Legal rules are unclear. Development authorities often have acquired additional land beyond that needed for infrastructure	There is no legal requirement about how excess land is sold or used and little transparency about the decision-making

Country or city	Type of land purchase	Rules for purchase and compensation	Rules or practice for acquiring excess land	Land sale procedure and use of proceeds
India (cont.)	purpose" and can also acquire land for priority industrial uses, including land that will be owned and developed by private owners or public-private partnerships.	can pass between notification and actual purchase date.	projects. Courts sometimes have ruled that takings were excessive.	process. Agencies are often reluctant to surrender control of land. However, increasing amounts of land are sold at auction.
Karachi, Pakistan	In the mid-1990s, land was expropriated by the government for development or redevelopment.	Compensation was set at 30% of the value of land in currently allowed use.	The process was hotly contested in the courts, tying up land for long periods of time.	There are no legal rules. The practice was to have public development of sites, often after substantial delay.
Dhaka, Bangladesh	In the mid-1990s, a municipality could request government to expropriate land for the municipal land development program.	Compensation was set at 150% of the market value of land (determined by the price of similar neighboring parcels). Structures were compensated at market value.	Government determined the amount of land that it was appropriate to take.	There are no rules and little transparency. Land was not sold, but remained in public hands after taking.

(continued)

Table 3.3 Rules for the Acquisition and Resale of Public Land in Select Asian Locations *(continued)*

Country or city	Type of land purchase	Rules for purchase and compensation	Rules or practice for acquiring excess land	Land sale procedure and use of proceeds
Hue, Vietnam	In the mid-1990s, land could be expropriated for the "benefit of the country."	The municipality initiated the request, which was then acted on by a higher authority. Compensation of land was based on an administrative formula, according to size and location of the plot.	In the three years preceding the survey, Hue expropriated about 8.2% of total land area of the city.	There is no legally prescribed procedure. Land was not sold but remained in public hands.

Source: Author's interviews; UNESCAP (1996); Ghosh (2006).

of golf courses as well as high-tech enclaves, which are able to benefit from a separate package of highly favorable tax advantages.

Public-private partnerships led by private partners tend to push the infrastructure envelope toward more aggressive development and sale of land. Bangladore's experience illustrates the risk that public authorities will back away from high economic returns in order to maintain bureaucratic control of development. The Department of Treasury of Karnataka State favored sale of the airport land retained by state agencies and use of the proceeds to finance public infrastructure projects that would facilitate airport access. However, the Karnataka State Industrial Investment and Development Corporation favored state construction of industrial facilities, ostensibly on the grounds that this would allow greater planning control over the character of development.[5]

Use of Eminent Domain

No aspect of urban development or infrastructure finance has become more controversial than government's use of eminent domain to acquire land. Aggressive use of government political power to acquire land at low prices has fueled popular resistance in China, India, and elsewhere. The issue is being addressed at the national level by legislation establishing clearer property rights and standards of compensation for compulsory land acquisition. International financial institutions also have begun to address the issue comprehensively, with particular attention to the rights of those displaced from their homes or workplaces by publicly sponsored land acquisition and development (for example, Azuela 2007; Bertaud 2007).

An emerging consensus holds that (a) the public sector has the right to acquire land for public investment projects, (b) compensation should be paid based on market value, (c) voluntary, negotiated land purchases are the preferred instrument for land transfers, (d) in the event that parties cannot agree on compensation, clear rules should apply for resolving differences, (e) occupants, including informal occupants, should be compensated as well as titled landowners, and (f) government should be prevented from compulsory acquisition of land for which it has no specific development plans. This consensus leaves unanswered two critical questions to be addressed differently in each country. First, how much surrounding land, not required for infrastructure construction, should public authorities be allowed to acquire under eminent

---

[5] Karnataka State Industrial Investment and Development Corporation's own calculations assume that state investment will take three years to complete construction and that facilities can be leased after four years, producing an 11 percent annual return on investment from the date of leasing.

domain? The public's ability to capture infrastructure benefits through the sale of land requires the ability to acquire some additional land, beyond that needed for infrastructure construction. However, the public's financial interest is likely to conflict with the interests of other parties. Second, what standards should be applied in determining "market-based" compensation? In particular, how much of the anticipated benefits from future infrastructure construction should be capitalized into the level of compensation that public authorities pay for land under compulsory acquisition? There is no universal answer to these questions, and different countries are developing policy along different lines.

Sale of Development Rights: São Paulo, Brazil

As an alternative to the sale of land to capture incremental value generated by public infrastructure projects, public authorities can sell development rights. Development rights fall into two categories: the right to convert rural land to urban use and the right to build at greater densities than normally would be allowed by zoning rules or height restrictions. Development rights of the latter kind normally are targeted at urban growth poles, like underground transit stations or other locations where higher-density development is appropriate. The essential equivalence between a development right and land is indicated by the Portuguese term *solo criado*—literally, created land—referring to the right to add floor space beyond the normal density restrictions for development.

São Paulo's sale of development rights illustrates the process (Froes and Robelo 2006). Like many other land-financing innovations, it had its origins in a municipal budgetary crisis that forced the municipality to look for off-budget resources to finance infrastructure investments. Under São Paulo's development regulations, developers do not pay a density fee for buildings that fall within the normal limitations on floor space. However, the municipality charges a preset fee for additional floor space (*solo criado*) beyond the normal maximum density, in locations authorized for higher-density development. Resources are dedicated to a special fund that can be used only to finance investment in works approved under the law establishing the respective urban operation.

The Faria Lima Urban Operation targeted a growth pole supported by the extension of Faria Lima Avenue and other public investments. Land values in the area reportedly have risen from US$300 per square meter, before public development, to US$7,000 per square meter afterward. In lieu of a betterment tax on land-value gains, the municipality offered to sell development rights for additional construction of 2.25 million square meters of floor space within the 410-hectare development area. Over the period of implementation, development rights have been sold for as much as R$1,100 (US$630) per square meter of allowable floor space. As of 2005 approximately 42 percent of the designated additional construction stock had been sold, for a total of R$320 million (US$190 million). Construction of a new metro stop at Faria Lima, started in 2005, promises to add to the value of the unsold development authorizations. Investment projects authorized under the urban operation include street improvements, an integrated drainage system for the area, public open space, and assistance for the construction of social housing.

Is there potential to generalize the approach? The World Bank proposed expanding the sale of municipal development rights to help finance the extension of metro line 4 and construction of the Feria Lima metro station. However, institutional relations have prevented this from happening. The metro is owned by the state government. The municipality of São Paulo controls land development rights and has preferred to use receipts from the sale of development rights to finance only infrastructure projects for which it has direct legal responsibility. Metro construction is being financed through conventional means, including international loans.

The potential exists for using land development rights to finance infrastructure construction on a much larger scale. In April 2007, the state of Maharashtra (India) approved a policy that will raise the maximum floor space index (FSI, the ratio of floor space to land area on a lot) throughout two of Mumbai's districts from 1.0 to 1.3. However, developers will have to purchase the extra FSI. For upper-income housing, the cost per square foot of additional building area will be set at 80 percent of the price per square foot of land in the assessment zone. The same policy is under consideration for application throughout the Greater Mumbai metropolitan region, which is projected to grow by 12 million to 14 million residents over the next 20 years. Sale of FSI rights in excess of the current 1.0 maximum ratio could yield several billion dollars of revenue and become the primary source of infrastructure financing for growth areas.

Developer Exactions and Impact Fees: Santiago, Chile

Although developer exactions and impact fees have become the most popular form of land financing for growth infrastructure in the United States, only developer exactions for internal infrastructure are common in the developing world. External exactions have been limited primarily to contributions of land that will be used for public streets, public parks, and other public facilities.[6] Santiago, Chile, appears to be the only metropolitan area that has experimented with impact fees designed to recover the differentiated costs of external infrastructure beyond the scale of local development (the following discussion draws largely on Zegras 2003).

As in the United States, impact fees were introduced at the local level in Chile primarily as a revenue-raising measure to finance needed infrastructure, against the background of highly constrained local financing options. Municipalities in Chile are prohibited from borrowing. They have only two significant types of own-source revenue: the property tax and vehicle registration fees. Tax and fee rates for both revenue sources are set by the national government, and 40 percent of local property tax collections and 50 percent of vehicle registration collections are transferred to the central government for redistribution through equalization grants. The capacity of rapidly growing cities to finance discretionary public works is highly constrained.

In the 1990s, two rapidly growing municipalities in the Santiago metropolitan region introduced impact fees on developers to finance roads linking subdivision development to the rest of the roadway network. These were ad hoc initiatives undertaken without national or regional authorizing legislation. Receipts were used to finance a large part of road construction.

At the end of the decade, impact fees were tried on a larger scale. Chacabuco Province, north of the consolidated metro region, emerged as a primary growth area that was going to be integrated into the metropolitan region. Fourteen major real estate projects were approved for development. They were expected to add 40,000 new households to the metro region by 2010. The projects were to be built on agricultural land lacking urban infrastructure services.

Developers were required to install at their own expense internal infrastructure systems. However, the projects were forecast to have significant impacts on the transportation network beyond the project development areas. A 21-kilometer radial highway connecting to the development region was to be built under the government's infrastructure concession program. An additional 41 kilometers of other roadways were to be constructed, as were several interchanges. The total impact (external costs) of new development on the regional road infrastructure was estimated at US$106 million. Because the proposed development involved multiple municipalities and because the scale of financing greatly exceeded local capacity, the national government took

---

[6] In Bogotá, 90 percent of the value of developer contributions has been in the form of land donations, despite the 1997 law that authorizes municipalities to impose betterment levies on the land-value gains created by planning authorizations for urban development. See also Tapananont and others (1998).

responsibility for planning the highway and negotiating the impact fee system with developers.

The impact fee formula that was adopted allocated costs among developers based on their location relative to the existing road network, project size, socioeconomic characteristics, and estimated travel demands. The original proposal called for all external costs to be financed through impact fees, with US$25 million paid to the concessionaire of the radial connector and the rest to the government. Travel demand originating in low-income housing units was exempted from the impact fee calculation and developer charges.

In the end, the government proceeded with implementation of the impact fee, but at a reduced rate. Government agreed to finance 39 percent of total costs from general revenues, with developer impact fees covering the remainder. The impact fee averaged about US$1,600 per housing unit.

Is Santiago's experience replicable? Santiago is a particularly favorable environment for piloting an impact fee experiment. Chile has for a long time (since the Pinochet regime) imposed developer exactions that require developers of middle-income housing to install or pay for internal infrastructure associated with subdivision development. The planning capacity of the government is well above average for developing countries, lending credibility to the analysis underlying estimates of the transportation impact of new development. Regulatory controls over land-use plans and subdivision development are relatively effective. Market principles are built into much of public service delivery, especially in the transportation sector, where extensive use is made of toll roads and private concessions for road construction.

Despite these favorable conditions, the impact fee experiment has not been replicated in Chile. One reason appears to be the reduction in financial pressure. Once investment responsibility was shifted to the national level, public authorities had a much wider range of financing options on which to draw. The financial constraints that drove innovation at the local level did not exist at the national level. Since large-scale development almost always crosses municipal boundaries, the national government is likely to be the principal player in future decisions about how road costs beyond the subdivision level should be financed.

The Chilean government continues to weigh the possibility of extending impact fees. If it does so, the next logical step would be to prepare national authorizing legislation that lays out the criteria for imposing impact fees, the principles for allocating costs among developers, and the levels of government that can impose such fees.

It is somewhat surprising that impact fees have not been adopted in other countries, given the financial pressures on infrastructure systems caused by rapid growth. One explanation appears to be that impact fees strike developers as direct costs without compensating benefits and therefore have been fiercely resisted. The "benefit" financed by impact fees is spread throughout the regional highway system and cannot be captured by the developer in land pricing. Alternative instruments, like the contribución de valorización or sales of serviced land to developers, are tied more directly to the developer's or landowner's gain. They appear as part of a mutual gain-sharing arrangement rather than as a pure developer cost.

A second explanation involves the planning expertise required to identify accurately and differentiate the off-site infrastructure costs caused by development in different locations. As a practical matter, wider application of impact fees in developing countries will require simplification of this process. A uniform development fee imposed on construction value, differentiated only by broad zonal characteristics—for example, near to or distant from existing infrastructure trunk lines—would capture the main principle of impact fees and lend itself to simpler administration.

4.

BALANCE SHEET ADJUSTMENTS AND LAND ASSET MANAGEMENT

The balance sheets of many public entities are top-heavy with urban land and property assets. At the same time, the cities where the property is located face severe shortages of infrastructure. Under these conditions, it can make sense for public authorities to exchange land assets for infrastructure assets. They do this by selling or leasing publicly owned land and using the proceeds to finance infrastructure investment. Rather than using land-financing instruments to finance individual investment projects, public entities undertake a balance sheet adjustment, in which they modify the overall composition of publicly held assets, increasing infrastructure assets and reducing land assets.

The public entity may be a municipality. Under some landholding regimes, all urban land is owned by the municipality and is available for leasing to private users. China is the preeminent example, but municipal ownership of all urban land is also found in Botswana and Ethiopia, among other countries, as well as in the city-states of Hong Kong in China and Singapore. In other cases, municipal governments for historical reasons own large amounts of urban land, including highly valuable, centrally located parcels. This is true of countries as varied as the Russian Federation and the Kyrgyz Republic, representative of countries of the former Communist bloc where new landownership laws have divided land into state, private, and municipal ownership, or the Arab Republic of Egypt and Vietnam, where historical particulars account for municipal holdings.[1]

---

[1] The World Bank's Urban Growth Management Initiative indicates that publicly owned land accounts for more than half of total city territory in 19 percent of the cities in its sample, including Algiers, Moscow, and Warsaw, and more than one-quarter of city territory in an additional 19 percent of cities, including Ho Chi Minh City, Istanbul, and Pusan (Rajack 2007).

Specialized public agencies also are significant owners of urban land. Often, these are urban development authorities that have the dual mission of investing in basic infrastructure and promoting urban economic development. The two missions can compete with each other for management attention and investment resources. As a result, development authorities of this kind often end up holding valuable parcels of land that either are not being developed fully as centers of economic activity or require so much capital for development that the core mission of infrastructure is being shortchanged.

One worldwide trend, seemingly in its early stages, is for municipalities, urban development authorities, and other public landholding agencies to adopt more active and more strategic methods of land asset management. This requires compiling an inventory of land and property holdings, assessing the economic potential of significant land parcels, and making strategic decisions about how land can best be developed or sold, given the constraints on public financing and the resource claims of infrastructure investment responsibilities.

This chapter illustrates the range of land asset management strategies and their potential for financing infrastructure investment—not only "municipal" investment but also infrastructure of interest for national economic development. Land asset management of this kind involves *privatization* through the sale or leasing of land. At the same time, responsibility for a greater part of project-specific infrastructure investment is shifted to the private sector owners. *Private participation in infrastructure investment* thus occurs at two levels: by helping to finance public investment through land sales and by transferring to private developers the responsibility for investment internal to major development projects.

None of these arrangements between the public and private sectors materialized overnight. The case studies illustrate the way public institutions have to evolve in order to make it feasible for them to dispose of land or property assets at market prices and to focus more on infrastructure investment.

Converting Municipally Owned Land to Municipal Infrastructure

The importance of land to public balance sheets is most pronounced in countries where municipalities hold land rights to all urban land. China and Ethiopia are two countries, at the opposite end of the income spectrum, operating under this type of landholding regime.

Unfortunately, municipal balance sheets are not available for public inspection in either country. In China, the local urban development and investment corporations (UDICs) that hold assets and borrow on behalf of municipal governments do not release their balance sheets even to rating agencies. In Ethiopia, municipalities do not prepare balance sheets or statements of assets. It is possible, however, to estimate the magnitude of municipal land assets, relative to municipal revenues, from the leasing prices for land and the amount of land held by municipal government available for release to the market. Table 4.1 summarizes such a comparison for Changsha, capital of Hunan Province in central China, as of 2002 (Peterson 2006). It shows that the net value of land available for leasing was roughly 14 times total municipal revenue in the same year. For comparison, the ratio of municipally owned land values to total annual municipal revenue was 0.38 in Dallas, Texas (chapter 2).

The massive municipal infrastructure investment in China over the past 15 years has been financed in large part by converting land assets into infrastructure. At least half of aggregate municipal infrastructure investment over this period has been financed by land assets, either directly through land leasing or indirectly through the use of municipal land to collateralize borrowing (Fu 2007; Ming and Quanhou 2007; Peterson 2007).

China's experience highlights some of the adjustments required to make land disposition work efficiently as well as some of the risks inherent in relying to this degree on land sales or land leasing for infrastructure finance. Originally, municipalities transferred land rights to developers primarily by private negotiation. In the mid-1990s, a review by the Ministry of Land and Resources found that more than 95 percent of all transfers had taken this form. Private negotiations with developers, however, opened the way for corruption and consequent revenue loss to government. In 2002, the central government promulgated a new circular instructing municipalities to lease landholdings through public auction. Although local governments did not change their practices overnight, follow-up audits found that a much larger share of land disposition took place through public auction and that leasing

Table 4.1   Importance of Land Assets in Changsha, Hunan Province, China, 2002

Indicator	Ratio
Ratio of gross municipal land value to municipal annual revenue	43.7
Ratio of land value available for leasing to municipal annual revenue	35.4
Ratio of potential net income from land leasing to municipal annual revenue	14.0
Dallas, TX: ratio of all balance sheet assets to municipal annual revenue	4.1
Dallas, TX: ratio of land assets to municipal annual revenue	0.38

Source: Peterson (2006).
Note: Net income from land leasing is after (a) resettlement costs for current occupants and (b) set-asides of land area for public use (streets, open space, and so forth).

prices for land sold at auction were considerably higher than those for land sold through private transactions.

Can China's experience be generalized? China is unique, both for its rapid and sustained growth and for the value of land held by municipalities. However, the core of its approach seems applicable elsewhere. Ethiopia has modeled its landholding regime after that of China, adopting public ownership of all urban land, assigning landholding rights to municipal governments, and encouraging land leasing as a way to generate capital revenue to finance infrastructure. National law requires that 90 percent of the proceeds from land leasing be used to finance municipal infrastructure investment. This requirement recognizes the one-time nature of up-front, land-leasing revenues. A recent review of municipal budgets has found that land leasing is financing between 50 and 100 percent of municipal infrastructure investment expenditures in a wide range of local governments (World Bank 2007).

Municipal and State Land Sales: Istanbul, Turkey

A more fundamental question is whether the sale or leasing of municipally owned land can be a significant source of capital revenue in places where private landownership is the norm. Very few municipalities have conducted land inventories to identify the land parcels they own, how they are being used, and their revenue-generating potential. The few exceptions point to the possibility that land assets can be a significant contributor to municipal capital budgets for a meaningful period of time.

Istanbul, Turkey, is a location where both the municipal government and state agencies have undertaken assessments of their excess landholdings that could be monetized to finance investment in infrastructure and moderate-income housing. The municipality's interest has been heightened by the difficulties it encountered in managing municipal debt. The Istanbul Metropolitan Municipality (IMM) in the 1990s borrowed extensively on international markets in foreign currency. When the Turkish lira fell precipitously in value, Istanbul was unable to repay its debts. The national government was forced to intervene by making payments on behalf of IMM and subtracting the payments from intergovernmental transfers to which IMM was entitled. The municipality's budget management in recent years has been aimed at reducing the reliance on borrowing and restoring the municipality's credit rating. The municipal government was able to reduce borrowing to 7 percent of consolidated cash receipts in 2006 and to improve its international credit rating from B+ to BB−.

Borrowing as a source of capital finance has been replaced by income from land and property sales. Table 4.2 shows the progression of receipts from such sales dedicated to the municipal capital budget. The municipality's proceeds for 2007 represent the sale of an old, central bus station for a price of US$17,856 per square meter, or a total of US$705 million (plus 18 percent value-added tax). The Roads Authority proceeds represent the sale of its district office property at a price of US$8,289 per square meter, or a total of US$800 million. In both cases, revenue from land sales has been dedicated to investment in transportation infrastructure. The amounts realized from land sales compare with Istanbul's total intermediate and long-term debt outstanding, used for capital purposes, of US$180 million at the end of 2006.

The 2006 and 2007 land sales are part of a program of planned disposition of assets, designed to accelerate new investment on centrally located sites and to generate income for public infrastructure investment. Istanbul's mayor has announced that the city intends to sell additional sites. In February 2008, the State Housing Development Authority announced that it intended to sell an old brewery site, most recently used as offices by the tax administration. Estimated proceeds are US$360 million, to be used to subsidize the purchase of moderate-income housing built by the Housing Development Authority.

Property sales of this magnitude, of course, cannot be sustained for a prolonged period of time. They represent a deliberate decision to exchange dormant land assets for badly needed transportation infrastructure and housing. In countries where municipal governments own a large volume of land, land sales can be a significant recurring contributor to capital budget financing. An examination of the financial statements of Alexandria, Egypt, for example, reveals that over the period 2000–05, land sales accounted for 20–30 percent of total local revenues. All proceeds from the land sales were dedicated to capital spending (Amin 2006). The importance of municipal-level land sales to the municipal budget and capital spending was greater in Cairo.

Often, however, publicly owned land in cities is not owned by municipal government, but by different agencies of the state or national government. This has made it difficult to match the proceeds from public land sales with the capital expenditure responsibilities of municipal governments, as revenue

Table 4.2 Public Property Sales in Istanbul, Turkey, 2003–07
(US$ millions)

Public authority	2003	2004	2006	2007
Municipality	4	66	640	705
Municipality plus Roads Authority	4	66	640	1,505

Source: For 2003–06, World Bank (2008); for 2007, press releases of Istanbul Metropolitan Municipality and the government of Turkey.
Note: US$1.00 = TL 1.24.

is retained by the selling agency and reinvested in infrastructure assets within its domain of responsibility. The following cases in this chapter examine this type of land disposition and infrastructure investment.

Transnet: Sale of the Victoria and Albert Waterfront in South Africa

Transnet is the South African national parastatal agency responsible for investment in transportation infrastructure. Its experience in divesting urban property holdings in order to concentrate financial resources and managerial attention on core infrastructure investment parallels that of the Port Authority of New York and New Jersey (chapter 2). It demonstrates the practical application of land sale as a tool of infrastructure finance as well as private participation in infrastructure finance via property development.[2]

Over the years, Transnet collected a wide array of urban landholdings through its subsidiary, Propnet. Some of these properties were part of urban redevelopment initiatives undertaken by Transnet at former transportation nodes. Other holdings consisted of excess land associated with major highway and rail networks. In 2004, as part of its strategy to increase basic infrastructure investment, the national government mandated Transnet to boost investment in transportation infrastructure, without the support of government grants or government subsidy. Under new leadership, Transnet set about transforming itself into a profit-making public enterprise with a greatly enlarged investment budget. As part of this redesign, Transnet undertook an assessment of the role and economic value of all of the assets on its balance sheet and launched a divestment (privatization) program to sharpen its focus.

In a transformative transaction executed in November 2006, Transnet sold the tourist and retail center it had developed on the Victoria and Albert Waterfront in Cape Town for R 7.04 billion (US$1.0 billion). The proceeds from this property sale were used to strengthen Transnet's capacity for basic infrastructure investment. Sales proceeds exceeded Transnet's entire fiscal 2006 nationwide investment expenditure and amounted to more than 17 percent of the total investment amount targeted in the new five-year investment plan that Transnet had prepared in collaboration with government. Table 4.3 summarizes the project.

Project History and Institutional Context

Transnet was created as a parastatal responsible for transportation infrastructure. Over time, it expanded into a large number of related and unrelated areas, including land development and property holdings through its subsidiary, Propnet. Early in this decade, government made the decision that

---

[2] See annual reports of Transnet at www.transnet.co.za.

Table 4.3 Summary of the Project to Sell Victoria and Albert Waterfront in South Africa

Executing authority	Project description	Sale agreement and proceeds	Use of funds for infrastructure
Transnet is the South African national parastatal responsible for managing and investing in transportation infrastructure.	Sale of Victoria and Albert Waterfront in Cape Town, which Transnet had developed from old docklands. The property contained 300,000 square meters of developed land and 250,000 square meters of land available for future development, all on the Cape Town waterfront.	Property was sold as freehold via international bidding. The sale to an international consortium was completed in September 2006 for R 7.04 billion (US$1.0 billion).	Government authorities announced the proceeds would be used to help finance Transnet's R 40.8 billion five-year capital investment program, with particular emphasis on modernization of rail freight and urban seaports. Part of the sale proceeds were received by Transnet's pension funds. The transaction strengthened Transnet's balance sheet for future borrowing by reducing net pension liabilities.

Source: Author.

Transnet should operate as a self-financing commercial entity, owned by government, but without government subsidy. Transnet was directed to prepare and execute a longer-term capital plan that would modernize and expand the country's basic transportation infrastructure networks supporting economic growth. As a result, Transnet and government developed both a five-year capital plan and a fundamental investment strategy. The investment strategy called for all new major highways to be built by the private sector as toll roads. Transnet would focus its investment efforts on modernizing the rail freight system, upgrading urban seaports for international trade, and installing pipelines.

A key part of Transnet's strategy involved identifying and assessing all of its far-flung holdings in order to identify noncore assets that should be divested, because they were being operated at a loss, because they could be managed more efficiently by the private sector, or because they commanded high market values that could be reinvested in core infrastructure functions. Following on this review, Transnet divested a large number of business units, including its share of South African Airways, passenger rail service, intercity bus service, an airport catering firm, information technology ventures, and other enterprises. Most of the entities were sold to the private sector (shares of South African Airways were transferred to government).

The most valuable noncore assets identified as a result of the review were land and property holdings held in the name of Transnet's subsidiary, Propnet. The single most valuable parcel was the Victoria and Albert Waterfront, developed from the old docklands in Cape Town. As owner of the docklands, Transnet began redeveloping the site in 1988, turning it into an international tourism and retail center, which in 2006 attracted 22 million visitors. The waterfront made an important contribution to the revitalization of Cape Town. However, as a tourist, commercial, and retail center, the project was tangential to Transnet's central transportation mission and could be developed further by the private sector.

Transnet and the government decided to sell the Victoria and Albert Waterfront through international bidding. Nine consortia qualified for the final short list, from a much larger number of interested parties. Bids were evaluated based on price (85 percent) as well as Black Economic Empowerment participation and protection of jobs for existing employees. The winning consortium was headed by London and Regional Group, a major international developer, and by Istithmar, a Dubai investment fund. South African Black Economic Empowerment groups represented 20 percent of the winning group. Current employees received a 2 percent property interest as well as guarantees of no job losses for two years. The sale price of the transaction was

R 7.04 billion (US$1.0 billion at the time), equal to more than 17 percent of the total investment laid out in the new five-year plan for Transnet's investment in transportation infrastructure.

Transnet pursued the sale as a direct result of its new mandate (a) to become a focused and efficient freight-moving organization, (b) to operate on commercial terms, not only without government subsidy, but returning a competitive rate of return to its owner, the government, and (c) to increase investment in basic infrastructure supporting its business activities. Divestment of noncore activities was a key to this focus. As Transnet's business plan asserted, "The present strength of the Group's balance sheet is undermined by the capital demands of its noncore assets."

Transnet chairman, Maria Ramos, noted at the time of sale, "We regard our holdings [in Victoria and Albert Waterfront] as a noncore asset, and its disposal for the maximum value is in line with our goal to raise cash for our infrastructure investment program … The sale of this shareholding will ultimately help us achieve our objective of transforming Transnet."

Transnet so far is well on its way to transformation and increased infrastructure investment. It has converted itself from a loss-generating parastatal into a profit-generating operation, transforming a R 6.3 billion annual loss into a R 6.8 billion profit. It increased its investment in transportation infrastructure from R 7.0 billion in fiscal 2006 to R 11.6 billion in fiscal 2007, and plans to invest R 16.9 billion in fiscal 2008. Proceeds from the sale of Victoria and Albert Waterfront of R 7.04 billion represent a significant contribution to the capital financing plan. In particular, the sale has strengthened Transnet's balance sheet, by reducing net pension liabilities (a portion of the waterfront was held in the name of Transnet's pension funds, and receipts were added to the pension fund's assets), allowing Transnet to enter the domestic bond market without government guarantee. In December 2007, Transnet issued R 2.5 billion in bonds, in an issue that was oversubscribed.

Transnet has updated and expanded its rolling five-year capital investment program, which now calls for R 78 billion in capital spending over the next five years, 2008–12, financed through R 25 billion in borrowing, with the rest financed through internal cash flows, including proceeds from property sales.

Prospects for Replication

Prospects for generalizing Transnet's experience in selling the Victoria and Albert Waterfront appear favorable. Transnet itself has identified other valuable urban properties that it will sell or contribute to joint ventures. The Carleton Center office building, in the heart of Johannesburg, as well as the former five-star Carleton Hotel are owned by Transnet and have been designated for sale through international auction. It is anticipated that the properties will fetch in the vicinity of R 1.5 billion or more. Transnet owns a large stretch of beachfront land along the N2 Highway in Port Elizabeth. The agency intends to convert this into financial value either through sale at auction or through a joint venture with a Port Elizabeth development authority that is trying to obtain government support for waterfront development along the lines of the Victoria and Albert Waterfront. In the latter option, Transnet would contribute land in return for a share of development profits. It appears that Transnet would prefer outright sale, but political discussions remain open about use of the Port Elizabeth waterfront land.

Transnet's policy of divesting noncore property holdings to increase infrastructure investment also is a practical model for other countries, especially those in Africa. Although the Victoria and Albert Waterfront is a uniquely valuable site, other publicly owned land held by government agencies has commensurate value relative to national and urban investment levels. In particular, national railroad companies and public port owners typically hold significant tracts of urban land that could be converted to more valuable use, while at the same time generating financial resources for investment in either transportation infrastructure or urban infrastructure more generally. A government mandate to inventory such land, assess its role in a focused transportation strategy, and sell excess landholdings for reinvestment in infrastructure assets could provide a significant boost to infrastructure budgets.

Mumbai Metropolitan Regional Development Authority: Bandra-Kurla Complex in Mumbai, India

India long has been troubled by a low rate of investment in urban infrastructure. Government has targeted the poor condition of urban infrastructure as a major constraint to continued national economic growth and has launched the Jawaharlal Nehru National Urban Renewal Mission (JN-NURM) as a national program to accelerate investment in cities' capital systems. Within the Indian governmental system, municipal governments have relatively little flexibility in the raising of revenue. Responsibility for infrastructure investment is scattered among various agencies, mostly controlled by state governments. Principal among these entities are states' urban development authorities.

The Mumbai Metropolitan Regional Development Authority (MMRDA) is representative of these development authorities. It is an agency of the state of Maharashtra, chaired by the minister of state for urban development, responsible for planning, development, and major infrastructure investment in the metropolitan Mumbai region. Metropolitan Mumbai had an estimated population of 17.7 million in 2001, projected to reach 30 million by 2020.

Faced with tight budget constraints and mounting investment requirements as part of Mumbai's economic development program, MMRDA, like other metropolitan development authorities, has recently turned to its land assets as a source of financing that can be reinvested in infrastructure.

The primary land parcel held by MMRDA is the Bandra-Kurla complex, for which it initiated development and is designated the special planning authority. MMRDA has begun to accelerate land sales from the complex. It now derives most of its income and capital resources from these land sales and has begun to focus more clearly on the investment uses to which land-sale proceeds will be put. The financial stakes are large. In just two land auctions, in January 2006 and November 2007, MMRDA was able to generate Rs50.8 billion (approximately US$1.2 billion) from the sale of small land parcels in Bandra-Kurla. This is almost 10 times total MMRDA infrastructure investment in 2004–05 and almost five times total infrastructure investment by the Mumbai Municipal Corporation in 2004–05. Table 4.4 summarizes the project.

Project History and Institutional Context

The Bandra-Kurla complex was developed by MMRDA starting in the late 1980s. It was created out of marshland and industrial slums by channeling the Mithi River and two creeks. The entire site occupies 553 acres and is being developed as an international financial, commercial, retail, and convention center with interspersed open space. Proceeds from the development—mostly in the form of annual rent payments and development fees—have been a primary source of income of MMRDA for years. However, proceeds have been scattered among numerous uses, without public accounting. Much of the income appears to have been used to support MMRDA's operating and staff expenses. Relatively small amounts have been dedicated to a revolving fund that supports subsidized infrastructure investment in towns throughout the state of Maharashtra.[3]

The decision to accelerate land sales from Bandra-Kurla, and in particular to emphasize *sales of land* rather than long-term leases of developed property built by MMRDA, was motivated by two factors. First, it was decided that Bandra-Kurla could be built out more efficiently by private developers. Individual land parcels within Bandra-Kurla are designated by MMRDA for specific development purposes—for example, five-star hotel, commercial

---

[3] Up to 2001, total proceeds from land sales, leasing revenues, and development fees at Bandra-Kurla were Rs17 billion. Total credits disbursed through the Maharashtra infrastructure revolving fund at that time were Rs624 million, with projects sanctioned for credit having a total loan value of Rs1.36 billion.

Table 4.4 Summary of the Bandra-Kurla Complex Project in Mumbai, India

Executing authority	Project description	Sale agreement and proceeds	Use of proceeds for infrastructure
Mumbai Metropolitan Regional Development Authority (MMRDA) is responsible for development planning and major infrastructure investments in Greater Mumbai region.	Bandra-Kurla is a 553-acre site, originally developed from marshland to be a secondary "suburban" commercial and office node to relieve congestion in central Mumbai. It has now become a valuable location for commercial activ ty and new commercial investment, rivaling the traditional economic center around the stock exchange.	Two successful land sale auctions took place in 2006–07. A total of 13 hectares of land were sold for approximately US$1.2 billion. However, in a 2008 auction only three of five parcels reached the minimum bid threshold. About 20 hectares of developable land remain available for sale.	Government authorities announced that sale proceeds would be used principally to finance MMRDA's capital investment plan, primarily the rail transit program being developed in collaboration with the World Bank under the Mumbai Urban Transit Project. However, there has been no disclosure or public commitment as to the exact use of funds.

Source: Author.

building of maximum floor space, convention center. The parcels are auctioned subject to this use restriction and then developed by the buyer. This public-private partnership has accelerated development relative to the former practice, where MMRDA constructed many of the properties and leased them to users in a finished state. The private developers at Bandra-Kurla are responsible for installing all access and on-site infrastructure at their own expense. The second factor motivating the sale of land was the desire to generate significant amounts of capital up front that could be invested in Mumbai's infrastructure.

Table 4.5 shows the history of land sales by MMRDA at Bandra-Kurla. The figures correspond to the highest price per square meter obtained in a land sale in the respective year. The table demonstrates the overall growth in land values, which greatly accelerated in 2006–07, as well as the cyclical nature of the urban real estate market. For a period after 1998, MMRDA suspended all land sales, as demand for urban space declined precipitously in the wake of the Asian financial crisis. In November 2007, one land parcel in Bandra-Kurla sold for Rs504,000 per square meter (more than US$12,000 per square meter of vacant land), the highest price recorded to date in India. Although typically described as land "sales," the transactions are actually 80-year leases.

MMRDA's use of land-sale proceeds to finance major infrastructure investment projects has involved an evolution in institutional practice. In the past, revenues from land sales and property leasing flowed into MMRDA's general budget. There was no public accounting of either receipts or uses of funds. In fact, infrastructure investment was not an especially high priority on MMRDA's list of responsibilities. MMRDA saw itself first as a planning

Table 4.5 Land Sales by Mumbai Metropolitan Regional Development Authority at Bandra-Kurla Complex in Mumbai, India

Year and use	Price per square meter
1993	Rs30,000
1995 (Diamond Bourse)	Rs42,500
1998	Sales suspended because of Asian financial crisis
2000 (Citibank)	Rs86,000
January 2006 (convention center)	Rs153,000
November 2007 (commercial complex and car park)	Rs504,000

Source: Author.

authority, responsible for preparing master plans and development plans; second as a planning coordination authority, responsible for guiding and approving private sector development so as to ensure its conformity with plans; and third as a special planning authority responsible for detailed land-use planning and implementation in notified areas, such as Bandra-Kurla.

Only in 2003 was the MMRDA Act amended to enable the authority to execute major infrastructure development projects within Greater Mumbai. The focus on infrastructure investment gave urgency to the sale of land in Bandra-Kurla, so as to generate funds to finance investment. MMRDA has announced that proceeds from the sale of land will be used primarily to help finance an urban transport program, which Mumbai has developed in collaboration with the World Bank, including an ambitious metro rail project scheduled to begin in 2008. There still is neither a public accounting for the use of funds, however, nor a publicly released budget that shows proposed sources and uses of funds for MMRDA capital projects.

Prospects for Replicability

Is MMRDA's experience replicable? The dramatic increase in urban land prices in India has mobilized much greater attention to the land assets held by urban development authorities and other agents of government, as well as the potential for converting land (via the market) into badly needed infrastructure. Within Mumbai, other government agencies have begun inventorying land and preparing it for sale. In November 2006, the national railway created a Rail Land Development Authority with the express purpose of identifying excess lands held by the railway that could be sold to help finance rail modernization. Sale of railway land within Greater Mumbai could help to finance part of the Mumbai rail connectivity plan. Urban development authorities (UDAs) elsewhere in India have begun to auction land, with the result that land sales have become the most significant element of UDA own-source capital revenues in large metropolitan areas.

Although it is commonly stated that the revenues from UDA land sales will be used for a combination of infrastructure investment and housing development, public accountability still is very weak. Undetermined portions of land-sale revenues continue to be used for UDA operating expenses. Neither the sources of funds for housing subsidies nor the amounts invested in infrastructure are clearly identified in UDA budgets. Efficiency and accountability in the development process would be greatly aided by transparent budgets, issued for public information, showing the sources and uses of funds, separate operating and capital budgets, and balance sheets summarizing the UDA's assets and liabilities.

An irony inherent in MMRDA's land sales, as well as that of most other development agencies, is that none of the proceeds inure to the benefit of the municipal government. The high-density development that takes place on such sites increases demand for municipal infrastructure services, such as water supply, wastewater collection, drainage, and street improvements. However, the UDAs are state institutions. They use their proceeds either to finance investment responsibilities within their own domain or to transfer funds to the state budget. The state of Rajasthan is an exception. Its legislation requires that 10 percent of all revenue generated from land sales within Jaipur metropolitan area, the state capital, go to the Jaipur Municipal Corporation to help finance municipal-scale infrastructure.

Land Auctions at the Urban Fringe: Cairo, Egypt

Egypt is characterized by highly concentrated development. Less than 5 percent of land in the country is arable and therefore traditionally suitable for either agriculture or urban development. The remainder of the land is desert. The limited supply of developable land has led to high land prices, exacerbated by large amounts of public landholdings and inefficient procedures for releasing public land for development.

As noted in chapter 3, Cairo is expanding rapidly into the desert hinterland, through a series of new towns and associated development. Expansion of the urban area is made possible by the extension of basic infrastructure systems, including water supply and road access. New town sites are designed by government planning authorities, but the investment in housing, commercial, and industrial development is carried out by private developers. Until recently, public land was transferred largely through private negotiation. Entities able to obtain land from the government, and secure development authorization, reaped huge windfall gains.

Project History and Institutional Context

In 2004, Egypt launched a Public Asset Management Initiative. To some degree, this relabeled a privatization program that had lagged expected performance and generated widespread social opposition. However, the new program (managed by the Ministry of Investment rather than the old Ministry of Public Enterprises) sought to undertake a comprehensive review of all assets held in the portfolios of different ministries. Its goal was to assess the economic role of each asset in helping the ministry to perform its core function and to determine if that function could be performed more efficiently by selling selected assets and redeploying the proceeds in activities that better fit the core mission. This approach shifted the perceived emphasis from what the private sector could gain by privatization of public assets to what the public sector could gain by better management of its assets, including the monetization of certain assets when in the public agency's interest. Public assets were to be sold through transparent, competitive means, including public auctions whenever feasible.

The Ministry of Housing, Utilities, and Urban Development's sale via auction, in May 2007, of land approved for development as part of new town development in East Cairo fit into this process. Land parcels were sold in large tracts for long-term development, one sale covering 6.3 million square meters, purchased by Damac Holding of the United Arab Emirates. Table 4.6 summarizes the project.

The ministry's land auction lies at the intersection of Egypt's asset management program and the government's program of new town development. Both of these programs reflect a commitment to enlarging the role of the private sector in economic activity, by focusing the public sector role on infrastructure investment, planning, and subsidy programs that allow the market to perform efficiently for persons of different income levels.

The asset management program was launched in 2004 under a new prime minister. All ministries and public agencies were instructed to conduct a thorough review of their asset holdings, make strategic decisions as to which assets could be divested as tangential to their primary mission, and how monetary receipts from sale could be reinvested most effectively. Proceeds from asset sales rose from £E 554 million in fiscal 2004 to £E 5.64 billion in fiscal 2005 and to £E 15.1 billion in fiscal 2006. Divestments included eight state-owned firms and the state's interest in 17 joint ventures, but the most common form of asset disposition was land sale. Forty sales of land or property were consummated by different ministries between 2004 and 2006.

The revenue-generating potential for land sales is illustrated by the May 2007 auctions. The £E 17.6 billion received from that month's land auctions were equal to approximately 10 percent of the entire national government budget and some 117 times annual nationwide collections from the property tax.

Prospects for Replication

Can Cairo's experience be replicated? The May 2007 land auctions are part of longer-term government policy that is certain to be replicated to a significant degree. Three of the land tracts scheduled for sale at auction in 2007, estimated to realize some US$1.6 billion, were withdrawn because bids did not meet the minimum asking price. They will be reoffered for sale. Land sales by national agencies also are taking place elsewhere in Egypt, as a means of raising capital for investment in irrigation, tourism development, housing, and

Table 4.6 Summary of the Land Auction Project in Cairo, Egypt

Executing authority	Project description	Sale agreement and proceeds	Use of proceeds for infrastructure
Ministry of Housing, Utilities, and Urban Development is responsible for new town planning and for construction of major highways and utility trunk lines. It owned the land sold at auction.	Sale at auction of desert land approved for development as part of new city development. Land was approved for a combination of housing and commercial uses.	Parcels were sold in May 2007 at rates that varied between £E 750 and £E 1,400 per square meter (US$140 to US$260). Total proceeds amounted to US$3.12 billion. Purchasers were largely land development entities from the United Arab Emirates and Saudi Arabia.	Private purchasers have responsibility for all internal infrastructure development. The Ministry of Housing announced that proceeds would be used for significant infrastructure investment, including construction of a four-lane access highway connecting to the Cairo Ring Road, and for housing subsidies for low-income households.

Source: Author.

industrial development zones. In fact, the World Bank in a policy note to the government of Egypt has found that the diversity of institutions selling public land, subject to widely varying rules and pricing regulations, stands in the way of orderly land asset management. It has recommended creating a single ministry that disposes of land according to a well-defined set of rules.

Like the other cases examined in this chapter, the land sales outside Cairo by national government have not generated revenues for the upgrading or extension of municipal infrastructure services in the existing city. The governates administering Egypt's cities do have significant landholdings of their own and have been mandated to go through the same type of land asset management program that is being applied at the national level.

Fort Bonifacio Land Sale and Development: Metro Manila, the Philippines

Bonifacio Global City is the culmination of an unusual public-private partnership in land development and infrastructure investment. Fort Bonifacio was a U.S. military compound until 1949, when it and other American bases in the Philippines were turned over to the Philippine government. Fort Bonifacio is located in a highly desirable part of Metro Manila, between two main international business districts, Makati and Ortigas.

In 1992, the Philippines passed Republic Act no. 7227, which had the purpose of "accelerating conversion of Military Reservations into other productive uses." The act authorized the sale of land, particularly of military compounds in Metro Manila, called for the conversion of Subic and Clark bases on Luzon Island into special economic zones, and created the Bases Conversion Development Authority (BCDA), which was given all the powers of an economic development and planning authority. In 1995 in what was termed the "Deal of the Century," the BCDA formed a joint venture with a private group to develop a 150-hectare portion of Fort Bonifacio. The BCDA sold a 55 percent stake in 150 hectares of Fort Bonifacio land for ₱30.4 billion (roughly US$800 million at the time) to the newly formed and jointly owned Fort Bonifacio Development Corporation. The private interest in Fort Bonifacio Development Corporation subsequently was sold to Ayala Land and a development subsidiary of Campos Group, two of the largest business organizations in the country. Villamor Air Force Base, also located in Metro Manila, was sold to other private parties.

Bonifacio Global City is the core development undertaking of the Fort Bonifacio Development Corporation. It has become a premier business district. Development, which initially was slowed by the Asian financial crisis, has accelerated rapidly in recent years. Table 4.7 summarizes the project.

Table 4.7 Summary of the Fort Bonifacio Land Sale and Development in Metro Manila, the Philippines

Executing authority	Project description	Sale agreement and proceeds	Use of proceeds for infrastructure
Bases Conversion Development Authority (BCDA) is charged with converting former U.S. military compounds to productive uses and is authorized to sell and develop former military land in Metro Manila.	BCDA formed a joint venture with private sector partners to develop part of Fort Bonifacio, the last remaining tract of large, undeveloped land in Metro Manila. The site is being developed as a high-end international business location, Bonifacio Global City.	BCDA sold 150 hectares of land to the newly formed joint venture, Fort Bonifacio Development Corporation, for ₱30.4 billion. BCDA also retained a 45 percent economic interest in the development joint venture, which is managed by the private partners.	The initial proceeds are allocated as follows: 50% for infrastructure investment in Subic and Clark special economic zones (SEZs), 32.5% for modernization of armed forces and military housing, 4% for housing for the homeless, 2.5% for the municipalities of Makati, Taguig, and Pateros, and 10% for the government's general budget. Infrastructure investment in Subic and Clark SEZs has now been completed, and BCDA is helping to finance a 94-kilometer four-lane highway connecting the two sites as part of Luzon regional development. The master plan for Bonifacio Global City calls for ₱8 billion in infrastructure investment over the next five years, to be financed by the joint venture developer.

Source: Author.

Project History and Institutional Context

The Bases Conversion and Development Authority Act represents a remarkable degree of development and planning foresight. Without legislative intervention, the undeveloped land of the military compounds likely would have been settled illegally. The BCDA is primarily an economic development program. In Bonifacio City, it has created a second international business center within Metro Manila. The two special economic zones (SEZs) financed by the program, Subic and Clark, have strengthened economic development in central Luzon. Most of the infrastructure investment financed by land sale has taken place either in central Luzon or in development of Bonifacio Global City. Few of the proceeds have leaked over to municipal-scale investment in basic services infrastructure.

As in almost all large land sales, controversies have arisen over the allocation of sales proceeds. The act creating the BCDA specified how the proceeds from the initial sales of land from Metro Manila military bases were to be allocated:

- Infrastructure investment in Subic and Clark SEZs: 50 percent
- Modernization of armed forces and military housing: 32.5 percent
- Housing for the homeless: 5 percent
- Shared among municipalities of Makati, Pateros, and Taguig: 2.5 percent
- General budget of government: 10 percent.

Most of the sale proceeds were deposited into the government treasury, leading to disputes as to whether the government then followed the allocation rules established by the BCDA Act. Military families, in particular, argued that they were inadequately compensated for having to leave military housing in the compounds. One organization of retired military personnel refused to leave military housing and sued the government in court over the issue. In January 2007, the Supreme Court of the Philippines issued a judgment that labeled the group as "professional squatters" and ruled that the law allows "summary eviction" when government infrastructure projects require conversion for development use.

Prospects for Replicability

Is the experience of Fort Bonifacio replicable? Within Metro Manila, experience to date is almost certain to be replicated and accelerated. Bonifacio Global City has successfully passed the take-off stage, with the development of numerous high-rise condominiums, commercial buildings housing international firms, a variety of international schools and educational institutions, a large, upscale shopping center, the Singapore embassy, and chic bars and clubs. Only a small portion of the site has been filled, with build-out scheduled to take place over the next decade. Development of other former military sites in Metro Manila is just getting under way, including the conversion of Villamor Air Base to a second international airport serving Metro Manila, with surrounding development.

The BCDA experience also holds promise as a model for other cities that have large military bases located within the urbanized area. Military property accounts for the largest share of publicly held land in such places as Delhi and Dhaka. Given the extremely high land prices in these areas, it is worth examining whether military functions could be performed equally well elsewhere, freeing up urban land for economic development.

5.

CONCLUSIONS, RECOMMENDATIONS, AND REFLECTIONS

Land-based financing has become an important element of urban infrastructure finance, especially in locations where cities are growing rapidly. The revival of land financing is so recent that it has attracted surprisingly little attention. Table 5.1 summarizes some of the land-financing cases reported in this book and compares the magnitude of financing with other sources of capital finance or total capital spending.

The potential advantages of land finance go beyond the generation of revenue. As part of the mix of capital financing, land-based financing complements borrowing. Most land-financing techniques generate revenue up front, thereby reducing the need for debt and the risks associated with future debt service. Several of the public authorities examined in this book—Cali (Colombia), Istanbul (Turkey), and Transnet (South Africa)—turned to land sales in part because they had incurred excessive debt and had lost access to the commercial debt market. Other cities were prohibited from borrowing by national regulations designed to reduce subnational financial risk. Even when local borrowing is feasible, up-front financing of infrastructure through land finance adds flexibility to the overall mix of capital financing.

A well-designed land-financing system also reinforces efficiency in urban land markets. Impact fees help to steer growth to where it can be accommodated most efficiently, by differentiating fee levels according to the additional

Table 5.1 Magnitude of Land Financing in Select Projects of Developing Countries

Location and activity	Land financing amount and use of proceeds	Comparative magnitude
Cairo, Arab Rep. of Egypt: auction of desert land for new towns (May 2007, 2,100 hectares)	US$3.12 billion: to be used to reimburse costs of internal infrastructure and build connecting highway to Cairo Ring Road	117 times total urban property tax collections in country; equal to approximately 10% of total national government revenue
Cairo, Arab Rep. of Egypt: private installation of "public" infrastructure in return for free transfer of developable desert land (2005–present)	US$1.45 billion of private investment in internal and external infrastructure plus 7% of serviced land turned over to government for moderate-income housing	Will provide a range of urban infrastructure services for more than 3,300 hectares of newly developed land, without financial cost to government
Mumbai, India: auction of land in the city's new financial center (January 2006, November 2007, total 13 hectares) by Mumbai Metropolitan Regional Development Authority (MMRDA)	US$1.2 billion: to be used primarily to finance projects in metropolitan regional transportation plan	10 times MMRDA's total capital spending in fiscal 2005; 3.5 times total value of municipal bonds issued by all urban local bodies and local utilities in India in past decade
Bangalore, India: planned sale of excess land to finance access highway to new airport built under public-private partnership	US$500 million plus: on hold; land apparently will be used instead for government office buildings and government-built industrial space	Minimum land-sale proceeds were estimated to exceed considerably the costs of highway construction and acquisition of right-of-way; present status: no access road to airport

(continued)

 Unlocking Land Values to Finance Urban Infrastructure

Table 5.1 Magnitude of Land Financing in Select Projects of Developing Countries *(continued)*

Location and activity	Land financing amount and use of proceeds	Comparative magnitude
Istanbul, Turkey: sale of old municipal bus station and former brewery used as administrative site (March and April 2007)	US$1.5 billion in auction proceeds to be dedicated to capital investment budgets	Total municipal capital spending in fiscal 2005 was US$994 million; municipal borrowing for infrastructure investment in 2005 was US$97 million
Cape Town, South Africa: sale of Victoria and Albert Waterfront property by Transnet, the parastatal transportation agency (November 2006)	US$1.0 billion, to be used to recapitalize Transnet and support its investment in core transportation infrastructure	Sale proceeds exceeded Transnet's total capital spending in fiscal 2006; equal to 17% of five-year capital investment plan prepared in 2006
Bogotá, Colombia: betterment fees, *contribución de valorización*	US$1.0 billion collected in 1997–2007; US$1.1 billion planned for 2008–15; used to finance city street and bridge improvement program	Finances 50% of street and bridge improvements; other sources of financing: US$50 million loan from the International Finance Corporation and US$300 million international, peso-linked bond issue

Source: Author.

infrastructure costs that must be incurred to deliver basic services to different development locations. As the cases reviewed in the book make clear, land sales by public authorities typically are motivated in equal parts by the desire to generate revenue for infrastructure investment and the desire to accelerate development of key projects central to economic development. An abandoned central bus station (Istanbul), reclaimed marshland (Mumbai), highly polluting industrial plants (China), or an empty military base (Manila) can become critical growth nodes through private investment. In all of these initiatives, there is a public-private partnership, in which the public sector exchanges land for revenue to finance public infrastructure investment *and* accelerate critical private investment. Finally, land-financing instruments establish market prices for land that help to guide efficient development of the urban area and can support development of the assessment base for property taxation.

Opportunities for Public Policy

Land financing is still in the early stages of development. The opportunities for national governments, local authorities, and international organizations to collaborate in more efficient design and implementation are numerous. Among the opportunities are the following:

- *Establish clear guidelines for public land auctions.* The financial amounts at stake in land auctions are large, and the difference between an efficient auction and an ad hoc auction, or no auction at all, is also large. The World Bank's assessment of urbanization in Ethiopia, for example, found that land leased at auction commanded prices 2 to 80 times higher than land sold through administrative negotiation. Land auctions in the Arab Republic of Egypt have increased proceeds from land sales by a factor of more than 10:1 from previous administrative sales of similar land. International organizations have helped countries to make more efficient use of the market on the procurement side of transactions, but much more could be done to support the efficient use of auctions in selling assets. There is now sufficient experience with land auctions in the developing world to put together best-practice guidelines for planning and conducting such auctions.
- *Prepare land asset management strategies.* Before selling land, municipalities and other public agencies should (a) carry out an inventory that identifies all publicly held land in an urban area, (b) establish the market value of significant parcels, and (c) make strategic decisions about whether parcels should be retained in current use by government, sold to the private sector, developed jointly by public and private partners, or converted to other public use. A track record has been established in places like Egypt and South Africa for conducting this type of strategic land asset management that can be tapped as the basis for establishing policy guidelines in other countries or urban areas.

- *Establish stable and equitable rules for the exercise of eminent domain.* The most controversial, and potentially destabilizing, aspect of urban land finance involves public acquisition of private or collective land through the use of eminent domain or other compulsory powers. The public sector's ability to finance infrastructure from increased land values depends, in part, on its ability to acquire more land than is required for the infrastructure project itself and, in part, on its ability to purchase land at a price that does not include capitalization of expected benefits from the infrastructure project. In the world of Henry George (1879, 1884) the increments in land values due to public investment were thought to belong clearly to the public, and thus subject to value capture by fiscal authorities. In today's world, the rights to incremental land values are highly contested. Farmers, developers, slum dwellers, and land speculators, as well as government, lay claim to the land-value gains created by public investment. The public sector's desire to maximize returns from the acquisition and sale of land has sometimes led to abusive condemnation procedures that ignore the claims of other parties. Clear laws that define how eminent domain can be used, the compensation that must be paid, and the procedures by which disputes will be resolved are critical to the continuing use of this type of land finance for infrastructure investment. By now, a good deal of experience has been accumulated in different countries on this issue, which it would be beneficial to compile and assess as preparation for national policy choices.
- *Identify workable modifications of betterment fees and impact fees as infrastructure financing instruments.* Colombia's modification of the contribución por mejoras points up the importance of making practical adjustments to traditional land-financing techniques so that they are workable under modern conditions. The next challenge is likely to involve the practical application of impact fees. Cities throughout the developing world are struggling to identify the kind of development fees that can be imposed on new construction both to defray some of the costs of infrastructure investment and to reinforce desired patterns of development.

Table 5.2 summarizes the different land-based financing instruments discussed in this book and the steps needed for their effective implementation. The instruments are listed in approximate order of real-world difficulty of implementation, from easiest to most challenging. Such an ordering, of course, is not universal. The feasibility of implementation of any technique will depend on the political context of a nation and on the legal precedents for using different types of land-based charges.

Table 5.2 Land-Financing Instruments

Instrument	Description	Key requirements	Overall difficulty
Developer exactions	Developer installs on-site and neighborhood-scale infrastructure at own expense	Clear regulations; planning and implementation capacity to link developer's infrastructure to public systems	Relatively straightforward
Sale or lease of publicly held land	Public land assets are sold, with proceeds used to finance infrastructure investment	Inventory of land assets, market valuation, and strategic decisions about best use; open auctions for disposing of land that is sold	Technical competence needed for initial inventory and appraisal; can be institutionally difficult when landholding agency does not benefit directly from sale
Public-private partnership: private investment in "public" infrastructure	Developer installs "public" infrastructure in exchange for land	Same information and analysis as for land sale; can accelerate private investment in key growth poles; competitive selection procedures become critical	Simpler than many other forms of public-private partnership; danger of nontransparent or corrupt deals between public sector and developer
Betterment levies	Public sector taxes away a portion of land-value gain resulting from infrastructure projects	Difficult and costly to administer on a parcel-by-parcel basis; simplified approach adopted by Bogotá holds great promise	Most appropriate for countries with a history of betterment levies—for example, Latin American countries in Spanish tradition

(continued)

Instrument	Description	Key requirements	Overall difficulty
Impact fees	Developers pay the cost of systemwide infrastructure expansion needed to accommodate growth	Strong planning and analytical capacity needed to identify infrastructure cost implications of development at different locations; strong execution of public investment plans	Need to develop simplified approaches that capture the core concept of recovering off-site costs of growth, without overwhelming technical demands
Acquisition and sale of excess land	Public sector acquires land surrounding the infrastructure project and sells land at a profit when project is completed and land value has been enhanced	Social agreement needed on who should benefit from land-value gains resulting from public infrastructure: the original landowner, the public fiscal authority, displaced occupants, other claimants	Technically one of the most straightforward options; the difficulty is to reach agreement on the proper exercise of eminent domain

Source: Author.

Risks and Limitations to Land Financing

It is good to end with a reminder of the risks and limitations of land-based financing of infrastructure. Three risks in particular deserve emphasis.

Urban land markets are volatile, and recent transactions may reflect a land asset bubble. Urban land prices in developing countries cannot steadily increase at 20–30 percent a year. Prices have been volatile in the past, and they will be volatile in the future. Land prices in developing-country cities now reflect worldwide economic conditions, ranging from the cost and availability of credit to the recycling of petro dollars. Of the transactions summarized in table 5.2, the land purchasers in Cairo, Cape Town, and Istanbul all were investors from Dubai, Qatar, or Saudi Arabia. In March 2008, the Mumbai Metropolitan Regional Development Authority held a land auction of Bandra-Kurla property, in which two of the five parcels offered for sale failed to meet the minimum pricing threshold, and prices declined from the November 2007 level. China's government has taken deliberate steps to cool urban land markets due to worries about excessive speculation and the impact on inflation.

Volatility in urban land prices is part of market reality. Practical protection against this risk starts by clearly identifying proceeds from land sales as one-time capital revenues that are used for one-time infrastructure projects. Risk is magnified when recent trends in land prices are extrapolated to prepare future years' capital investment plans and is magnified still further if part of the receipts from land financing is allowed to trickle over to finance operating budgets.

Land sales often lack transparency and accountability. The majority of land sales are conducted off budget. There is little public accountability as to how revenues are used. The great sums of money involved invite corruption and institutional capture by the selling agency, without regard to other priorities. This risk can be mitigated by publicly releasing capital budgets and balance sheets, which report on agencies' sources and uses of funds, including those generated by land transactions. Special legislation that earmarks the revenues from land sales for capital investment can protect receipts from being diverted to operating budgets. Laws that require publicly owned land to be sold at public auction reduce the potential for corrupt deals with private land developers.

Special measures may need to be taken to make land-based financing support investment in basic municipal services. As the cases in this book illustrate, land financing has most often been used to finance urban transportation projects or the infrastructure required to service new development at the urban fringe. It has been used less frequently to finance investment in existing basic infrastructure services, such as repair or upgrading of water supply, waste-water collection, or solid waste removal. One reason is that water supply agencies and other basic services agencies, unlike transportation agencies or development authorities, typically do not own excess land that can be sold or developed. Where municipal government is responsible for providing the full range of infrastructure services, this distinction is less important. Budgets are fungible, and the fact that land financing helps to pay for particular investment projects should free up other funds for investment in basic services. However, experience demonstrates that the institutional owners of public land are reluctant to share sale proceeds with others, including other agencies in the same government. The solution to this risk lies either in governance reform, which establishes a consolidated capital budget, or in a sharing agreement that automatically allocates a part of land finance proceeds to the municipal government responsible for the delivery of basic services.

REFERENCES

Altschuler, Alan A., and José A. Gómez-Ibáñez, with Arnold M. Howitt. 1993. *Regulation for Revenue: The Political Economy of Land Use*. Washington, DC: Brookings Institution.

Amin, Khaled. 2006. "Alexandria Fiscal Profile." Report prepared for the World Bank, Washington, DC.

Archer, R. W. 1976. "The Sydney Betterment Levy, 1969–1973: An Experiment in Functional Funding for Metropolitan Development." *Urban Studies* 13 (3): 339–42.

Atisreal and Geofutures. 2005. "Property Values Study: Assessing the Changes in Value Attributable to the Jubilee Line Extension." Report prepared for Transport for London.

Azuela, Antonio, in collaboration with Carlos Herrera. 2007. "Taking Land around the World: International Trends in the Expropriation of Land for Urban and Infrastructure Projects." Paper presented at World Bank, Urban Research Symposium, "Urban Land Use and Urban Land Markets," Washington, DC. May.

Barker, Kate. 2004. *Review of Housing Supply*. London: Her Majesty's Treasury.

———. 2006. *Review of Land Use Planning*. London: Her Majesty's Treasury.

Bertaud, Alain. 2007. "Land Leasing and Sales to Finance the Capital Cost of Infrastructure in China and Elsewhere: Implementation Issues." World Bank, Washington, DC.

Bowles, Liza K., and Arthur C. Nelson. 2007. *Impact Fees: Equity and Housing Affordability; A Guidebook for Practitioners*. Washington, DC: U.S. Department of Housing and Urban Development.

Brueckner, Jan K. 1997. "Infrastructure Financing in Urban Development: The Economics of Impact Fees." *Journal of Public Economics* 66 (3): 383–407.

———. 2001. "Urban Sprawl: Lessons from Urban Economics." In *Brookings-Wharton Papers on Urban Affairs: 2001*, ed. William G. Gale and Janet Rothenberg Pack. Washington, DC: Brookings Institution.

Burrows, Edwin G., and Mike Wallace. 1999. *Gotham: A History of New York City to 1898*. New York: Oxford University Press.

City of Phoenix, Arizona. 2006. *Infrastructure Financing Plan for the Development Impact Fee Areas*. Phoenix, AZ: City of Phoenix. November. http://www.phoenix.gov/PLANNING.

Doig, Jameson W. 2001. *Empire on the Hudson: Entrepreneurial Vision and Public Power; The Port Authority of New York*. New York: Columbia University Press.

Duncan Associates. 2007. National Impact Fee Survey, 2007. http://www.impactfees.com.

El Kovedia, Hazem, and Mostafa Madbourly. 2007. "Tackling the Shelter Challenge of Cities: Cairo, Egypt." World Bank, Washington, DC.

Froes, Marilda, and Jorge M. Robelo. 2006. "Urban Operations and the São Paulo Metro Line 4." Paper prepared for the World Bank, Washington, DC.

Fu, Gao Guo. 2007. "Urban Infrastructure Investment and Financing in Shanghai." In *Financing Cities: Fiscal Responsibility and Urban Infrastructure in Brazil, China, India, Poland, and South Africa*, ed. George E. Peterson and Patricia Clarke Annez. London: World Bank and Sage Publications.

Furtado, Fernanda, and Pedro Jorgenson. 2006. "Value Capture in Brazil: Issues and Opportunities [in Portuguese]." Report prepared for the World Bank, Washington, DC.

Gdesz, Miroslaw. 2005. "Adjacency Levies in Poland: Main Problems." Paper presented to the conference "From Pharaohs to Geoinformatics," Global Spatial Data Infrastructure, Cairo, Egypt. April.

George, Henry. 1879. *Progress and Poverty*. Reprint, New York: Robert Schalkenbach Foundation, 1987.

———. 1884. *The Land Question*. Reprint, New York: Robert Schalkenbach Foundation, 1987.

Ghosh, Asha. 2006. "Banking on the Bangalore Dream." *EPW Commentary*, February 25.

Gihring, Thomas A., and Jeffrey J. Smith. 2006. "Financing Transit Systems through Value Capture: An Annotated Bibliography." *American Journal of Economics and Sociology* 65 (3, July): 751–86.

Hagman, Donald G., and Dean J. Misczynksi, eds. 1978. *Windfalls for Wipeouts: Land Value Capture and Compensation*. Washington, DC: Planners Press.

Harvey, David. 2003. *Paris, Capital of Modernity*. Paris: Routledge.

Hass-Klau, Carmen. 2006. "Evidence of Price Premiums at Public Transport Stations in Several European Metropolitan Areas." University of Wuppertal, Germany.

Heim, Carol E. 1990. "The Treasury as Developer-Capitalist? British New Town Building in the 1950s." *Journal of Economic History* 58 (4, December): 903–24.

Henao González, Gloria. 2005. "Instrumentos para la recuperación de plusvalías en Bogotá." *Café de las ciudades* 4 (35, September): n.p.

Hong, Yu-Hung, and Barrie Needham, eds. 2007. *Analyzing Land Adjustment: Economics, Law, and Collective Action.* Cambridge, MA: Lincoln Institute of Land Policy.

IFC (International Finance Corporation). 2008. "Bogotá Street Rehabilitation: Summary of Proposed Investment." IFC, Washington, DC.

Ingram, Gregory K. 2007. "Prioridades para el desarrollo urbano." Paper presented at the "Seminario 10 años de la ley 388 de 1997: Sus aportes al ordenamiento y de la consolidación de política de suelo," Universidad Nacional de Colombia, Instituto de Estudios Urbanos, Bogotá. May 24–25. http://www.territorioysuelo.org.

Jaramillo, Samuel. 2001. *The Betterment Levy and Participation in Land Value Increments: The Colombian Experience.* Cambridge, MA: Lincoln Institute for Land Policy.

Jones Lang LaSalle. 2004. "Land and Property Value Study: Assessing the Change in Land and Property Values Attributable to the Jubilee Line Extensions." Report prepared for Transport for London.

Kaganova, Olga, and James McKellar, eds. 2006. *Managing Government Property Assets: International Experiences.* Washington, DC: Urban Institute.

KPMG. 2006. *India's Airports: Now Boarding for Growth.* Mumbai: KPMG.

Marchand, Bernard. 1993. *Paris: Histoire d'une ville; XIXe–XXe siècle.* Paris: Editions du Seuil.

Massa-Gille, Geneviève. 1973. *Histoire des emprunts de la ville de Paris (1814–1875).* Paris: Commission des Travaux Historiques.

Mikkelson, Jans Kramer. 2007. "Orestad, the Generator of the Oresund Region." Udenrigsministeriat, Copenhagen.

Ming, Su, and Zhao Quanhou. 2007. "China: Fiscal Framework and Urban Infrastructure Finance." In *Financing Cities: Fiscal Responsibility and Urban Infrastructure in Brazil, China, India, Poland, and South Africa,* ed. George E. Peterson and Patricia Clarke Annez. London: World Bank and Sage Publications.

Mitchell, Stephen R., and Anthony J. M. Vickers. 2003. "The Impact of the Jubilee Line Extension on Land Values." Working Paper 035M1, Lincoln Institute of Land Policy, Cambridge, MA.

Orestad Corporation. 2005. *Annual Report 2005.* Copenhagen: Orestad Corporation.

———. 2006. *Annual Report 2006.* Copenhagen: Orestad Corporation.

———. 2007. *Annual Report 2007.* Copenhagen: Orestad Corporation.

Peterson, George E. 2005. "Report and Recommendations on Municipal Finance Situation in Amhara and Tigray Regions." Report prepared for the World Bank and government of Ethiopia, Urban Institute, Washington, DC.

———. 2006. "Municipal Asset Management: A Balance Sheet Approach." In *Managing Government Property Assets: International Experiences,* ed. Olga Kaganova and James McKellar. Washington, DC: Urban Institute.

————. 2007. "Land Leasing and Land Sale as an Infrastructure Financing Option." In *Financing Cities: Fiscal Responsibility and Urban Infrastructure in Brazil, China, India, Poland, and South Africa,* ed. George E. Peterson and Patricia Clarke Annez. London: World Bank and Sage Publications.

Pinkney, David. 1957. "Money and Politics in the Rebuilding of Paris, 1860–1870." *Journal of Economic History* 17 (1, March): 45–61.

Port Authority of New York and New Jersey. 2005. *Annual Report for 2005.* http://www.panynj.gov.

————. 2006. *Annual Report for 2006.* http://www.panynj.gov.

————. 2007a. *Annual Report for 2007.* http://www.panynj.gov.

————. 2007b. *Updated 2007–2016 Capital Investment Plan.* http://www.panynj.gov.

Rajack, Robin. 2007. "Does the Ownership and Management of Public Land Matter to Market Outcomes?" Paper presented to the Urban Symposium "Urban Land Use and Urban Markets," World Bank, Washington, DC.

Riley, Don. 2002. *Taken for a Ride: Trains, Taxpayers, and the Treasury.* London: Centre for Land Policy Studies.

Rojas Rojas, Arturo Fernando. 2007. "Ley 388 de 1997: Una caja de herramientas para la construcción de un territorio común: Lecciones y aprendizajes de la experiencia de Bogotá." Paper presented at the conference "Seminario 10 años de la ley 388 de 1997: Sus aportes al ordenamiento urbano y a la consolidación de políticas de suelo," Universidad Nacional de Colombia, Instituto de Estudios Urbanos, Bogotá. May 24–25. http://www.territorioysuelo.org.

RTI International. 2005. "Case Study on Mobilization of Private Capital in Bogotá, Colombia." Report prepared for the World Bank Municipal Task Force, Washington, DC.

Saldies Barrenocha, Carmenza. 2007. "El ordenamiento territorial en Bogotá." Paper presented at the conference "Seminario 10 años de la ley 388 de 1997: Sus aportes al ordenamiento urbano y a la consolidación de políticas de suelo," Universidad Nacional de Colombia, Instituto de Estudios Urbanos, Bogotá. May 24–25. http://www.territorioysuelo.org.

Salheen, Mohammed. 2006. "Cairo, Egypt." Presentation to the International Symposium "New Towns as a Concept for Sustainable Development of Megacity Regions?" Berlin Technische Universitat, September.

Schafer, Rudolf. 2006. "New Towns as a Decongestion Strategy for Megacity Regions? The Cases of London and Cairo." Paper presented at the conference "New Towns as a Concept for the Sustainable Development of Megacity Regions?" Berlin Technische Universitat, September.

Secretariat of the Committee on Infrastructure. 2006. *Financing Plan for Airports.* Delhi: Government of India.

Serra, M. V., David Dowall, and D. M. da Motta. 2003. *Análise do mercado de solo urbano em metrópoles do Brasil: Recife.* Washington, DC: World Bank, Cities Alliance, Instituto de Pesquisa Econômica Aplicada, and Fundação de Desenvolvimento Municipal.

Smolka, Martim. 2007. "La regulación de los mercados de suelo en América Latina: Cuestiones claves." Paper presented at the "Seminario 10 años de la ley 388 de 1997: Sus aportes al ordenamiento urbano y la consolidación de políticas de suelo," Universidad Nacional de Colombia, Instituto de Estudios Urbanos, Bogotá. May 24–25. http://www.territorioysuelo.org.

Tapananont, Napanant, Premsiri Kaseman, Sansance Srisukre, and Jarunan Suthiprapa. 1998. "A Case Study on Development Exaction for Distributor Road Construction in Bangkok." In *Proceedings of the Second International Expert Panel Meeting on Urban Infrastructure Development,* ed. Andrea Czarnecki, 347–63. Nagoya, Japan: United Nations Centre for Regional Development.

United Kingdom, Her Majesty's Treasury. 2006. *Government Response to the Communities and Local Government Committee's Report on the Planning Grant Supplement.* London: Her Majesty's Treasury.

United Nations. 1976. *Report of Habitat: United Nations Conference on Human Settlements, Vancouver, 31 May–11 June 1976.* Geneva: United Nations.

UNESCAP (United Nations Economic and Social Commission for Asia and the Pacific). 1996. *Municipal Land Management in Asia: A Comparative Study.* Bangkok: UNESCAP.

Vickrey, William S. 1997. "The City as a Firm." In *The Economics of Public Services,* ed. Martin S. Feldstein and Robert P. Inman. London: Macmillan.

Wahba, Samah. 2007. "Management of Public Land Assets in Egypt: Improving Fiscal and Economic Benefits of Land Disposition." World Bank, Washington, DC.

World Bank. 2006. *Egypt Public Land Management Study.* 2 vols. Washington, DC: World Bank.

———. 2007. "Ethiopia Urbanization Study." Draft. World Bank, Washington, DC.

———. 2008. "Turkey: Istanbul Financial Note." World Bank, Washington, DC.

Yiu, C. Y. 2005. "The Effects of Expected Transport Improvements on Housing Prices." *Urban Studies* 42 (1): 113–25.

Zegras, Christopher. 2003. "Financing Transport Infrastructure in Developing Country Cities: Evaluation of and Lessons from Nascent Use of Impact Fees in Santiago de Chile." *Transport Research Record* 1839 (April): 81–88.

INDEX

Boxes, figures, notes, and tables are indicated by *b, f, n,* and *t,* respectively.

A

accelerated generation of revenue via
land-based financing, 29, 103
accountability and transparency issues,
12, 110
acquisition and sale of private land.
See eminent domain; value capture
via land sale
ADC (Andean Development Corporation),
63–64
airports
Heathrow Airport, London, Crossrail
access to, 25, 31, 69*n*3
India, airport construction in, 3*t*, 8, 25,
68–75, 69*t*
Alexandria Company for Urban
Development, 60*b*
Alexandria, Egypt, 85
Algiers, Algeria, 81*n*1
Andean Development Corporation (ADC),
63–64
Arab Republic of Egypt. *See* Egypt, Arab
Republic of
Argentina, 64
Asia. *See also* specific countries
development with rudimentary

infrastructure in, 32–33
financial crisis (1997), 28, 93*t*, 98
land acquisition rules in, 71, 72–74*t*
land readjustment schemes in, 6, 31,
42, 59
auctions of public land, 11, 58, 96–98,
97*t*, 106
Australia (Sydney), betterment levies in,
38, 39–40I
Ayala Land, 98

B

balance sheet adjustment, land asset
management as, 10, 21, 48–50,
49*t*, 81
Bandra-Kurla complex, Mumbai, India,
3*t*, 90–95, 92*t*, 93*t*, 104*t*, 110
Bangalore, India, greenfield international
airport, 3*t*, 8, 25, 68, 69–75, 69*t*,
104*t*
Bangladesh, 73*t*, 101
Barranquilla, Colombia, 64
Bases Conversion Development Authority
(BCDA), Philippines, 98–101, 99t
basic urban services, land-based financing
for, 23*t*, 25–26, 110–11
BCDA (Bases Conversion Development
Authority), Philippines, 98–101, 99*t*
benefit capitalization, 32–33

land acquisition rules in, 72*t*

land asset management in, 50, 81,
82–84, 83*t*

municipal ownership of urban land in,
81, 82–84, 83*t*

polluting industrial plants, conversion
of, 5, 105

profit maximizing in, 28

scale and magnitude of land-based
financing in, 20

time limitations on land-financing
strategies, 12

UDICs, 82–83

value capture via land sale, 8, 66–68

volatility of land market, attempts to
cool, 110

Clark base, Luzon Island, Philippines,
98, 100

collateralization of public land, 68

Colombia

betterment levies in

Barranquilla, 64

Bogotá, 4*t*, 6–7, 61–64, 62*t*, 65*b*,
78*n*6, 105*t*

Cali, 62*t*, 64, 65*b*, 103

Medellín, 64

modification of, 11, 63, 107

road and highway improvements in
Bogotá, 4*t*, 105*t*

*contribución de valorización/contribución
por mejoras. See* betterment levies

contributions, voluntary or negotiated,
38–41, 45*n*2

corruption, x, 12, 28, 83, 110

cost recovery techniques. See developer
exactments; impact fees

created land (solo criado), 76

Crossrail commuter system, London, 25,
40–41

cyclical nature of urban land market, 12,
27–28, 110

D

Dallas, Texas, land asset management in,
49–50, 49*t*, 83*t*

Damac Holding, 96

Delhi, India

airport modernization, 68, 69*t*

metro authority, 41

military property in, 101

Denmark, new community of Orestad
in, 7, 33–34, 34–35*b*, 56

density regulations, 28–29

developed countries, land-based financing
for urban infrastructure in, 31–50.
See also specific cities and countries
by name

benefit capitalization, concept of,
32–33

betterment levies, 36–38, 39–40*b*

developer exactions in, 45

developer land sales, 33–35

eminent domain in, 42, 66

historical instances, x, 1–2, 17–18, 26,
31, 33, 42, 43–44*b*

impact fees in, 6, 9–10, 31, 45–48, 47*b*,
77–78

importance of studying, 5–6

land asset management, 48–50, 49*t*,
51–54*b*

negotiated or voluntary contributions,
38–41, 45*n*2

new town development in, 33–35,
34–35*b*

value capture, concept of, 32–33,
35–36

value capture via land sale, 41–44,
43–44*b*

developer exactions, 9, 14*t*, 108*t*

in developed countries, 45

in developing countries, 77

economic efficiency of, 22–23

developer land sales, 7, 14*t*, 108*t*

in developed countries, 33–35, 34–35*b*

in developing countries, 56–61, 60*b*

developing countries, land-based financing
for urban infrastructure in, 55–80.
See also specific cities and countries
by name

betterment levies, 4*t*, 6–7, 11, 61–64,
62*t*, 65*b*, 78*n*6

developer exactions, 77

developer land sales for new towns,
56–61, 60*b*

development rights, sale of, 9, 76–77

ECO-AUDIT
Environmental Benefits Statement

The World Bank is committed to preserving endangered forests and natural resources. The Office of the Publisher has chosen to print *Unlocking Land Values to Finance Urban Infrastructure* on recycled paper with 30 percent postconsumer fiber in accordance with the recommended standards for paper usage set by the Green Press Initiative, a nonprofit program supporting publishers in using fiber that is not sourced from endangered forests. For more information, visit www.greenpressinitiative.org.

Saved:

• 6 trees

• 27 million British thermal units of total energy

• 4,097 pounds of net greenhouse gases

• 13,300 gallons of waste water

• 1,570 pounds of solid waste